HANCHER VS. HILTON

Also by Matt Kuhns

*Brilliant Deduction: The Story of
Real-Life Great Detectives*

*Cotton's Library:
The Many Perils of Preserving History*

HANCHER VS. HILTON

Iowa's Rival University Presidents

Matt Kuhns

Lyon Hall Press
Lakewood, Ohio

Copyright © 2016 by Matthew John Kuhns

All rights reserved. No part of this book may be used or reproduced in any manner whatsoever without written permission from the publisher except in the case of brief quotations embodied in critical articles or reviews.

Published in the United States by Lyon Hall Press, Lakewood, Ohio

Every reasonable effort has been made to respect the owners of material reproduced in this book, but if any rights have been overlooked, the author and publisher welcome notification of the error.

Library of Congress Control Number: 2016912389

ISBN-13: 978-0-9882505-7-4

Printed on acid-free paper

Designed and typeset by Modern Alchemy LLC

For my father

CONTENTS

Introduction 1
Locations 10
A note on names 11
1. The Scholar 13
2. The Salesman 37
3. Hilton's Dream 53
4. Collegiality 67
5. Rupture 75
6. A Matter of Identity 91
7. Marking Territory 99
8. Halftime 121
9. Educational Load Factor 135
10. Miscalculations 151
11. Irreconcilable Differences 167
12. Showdown 187
13. Legacies 205
14. Evaluation 221
Acknowledgements 239
Select Bibliography 241
Notes 245
Index 267

INTRODUCTION

"Academic men quarrel as readily as men in other sectors of society. Since they persuade themselves more easily that they are standing up for a principle, they can be vigorous and sometimes cruel combatants."[1]
— C. W. De Kiewiet, fifth president of the University of Rochester

When a university's president proposes dismantling and absorbing the institution's traditional rival, it makes news. It constitutes, by general consensus, a big story.

It's no real mystery, therefore, how an unheralded weekday morning meeting of service clubs in Iowa City, in early 1964, not only made the 10 o'clock news[2] but kicked off days of press coverage, angry rebuttals, and eventually a frantic intervention by Iowa's governor. President Virgil Hancher was advocating, essentially, the dismemberment of Iowa State University.

No milder term seems adequate to Hancher's proposal of January 29, 1964. The University of Iowa president called for combining all Iowa's public colleges into a single university system, as he had already proposed several years earlier to a firmly negative reception. For the state's other full-fledged university, Iowa State, Hancher now offered an even more audacious prescription. The universities' common governing board, he suggested, should expand the role of land-grant institution from

Iowa State to both schools.³ Then, once equally qualified for lucrative state and federal programs tied to land-grant status, the University of Iowa could assume control of its rival's statewide off-campus extension service alongside its own, smaller extension division, and perhaps that of the state's third college in Cedar Falls. The three programs were poorly coordinated at present, Hancher argued, and would inevitably develop costly redundancies absent a single authority in charge. As the population was moving away from the agricultural economy toward which Iowa State's extension was geared, transferring it to the more urban and broad-based University of Iowa would neatly solve two problems.⁴

Iowa State University's president James Hilton saw the issue rather differently, to say the least. Hilton had spent his life among America's land-grant colleges, beginning as a freshman at North Carolina State 45 years earlier and continuing through a distinguished career that culminated at ISU. In between, he had also contributed to the ISU Extension firsthand as a county agent in the 1920s. Hilton revered Iowa State, and extension, as the best examples of a century-old tradition of placing higher education at the service of all the state's people. Hancher's proposal to remove these attributes and reduce Iowa State to a University of Iowa branch campus was appalling to Hilton, even absurd. Yet it was also probably something less than a genuine shock.

By 1964, Hancher and Hilton had clashed again and again for several years. They fought over broad policy and minor details, over curriculum, and funding, and even charges of unconstitutionality. They argued in meetings, in memos, and

INTRODUCTION

repeatedly in public statements; rumors of personal animosity and petty acts of sabotage, behind the scenes, seemed credible if unsubstantiated. Though Iowa State and Iowa were inherently rivals in some sense from their very creation, the battles of Hancher vs. Hilton were something else. Through these years—during which the schools did not meet in athletic matches at all—institutional conflict narrowed to a one-on-one contest. Rivalry, meanwhile, expanded to a struggle for existence.

A born-and-raised Iowan and alumnus of Iowa State University, for many years I supposed that I understood college rivalry in Iowa as well as all but the most dedicated trivia fans. So far as I knew there was little that would not be generally familiar to anyone in the United States, for that matter, simply because Iowa's college rivalries seem entirely ordinary. In 2002, veteran sportswriter Frank Deford produced what I imagined would be the definitive statement on the topic. Declaring himself, as a rule, a fan of any "State University," Deford explained this as his way of cheering the underdog:

> State colleges invariably were created after the "University of" colleges. Usually the "University of" colleges are the more hoity-toity places. They like to call themselves "the flagships," *ooh*. In fact a lot of state colleges started out as agricultural schools, "Aggies," like they were marbles. So stuck-up fans of the aristocratic University schools would all go "mooo!" during games and holler other nasty barnyard things. […]

> Whatever the original reasons, schools with "State" in their name never have the cachet that the "Universities of" have. So, as a lover of underdogs, I always root for the state colleges.[5]

This more or less described public higher education in Iowa as I have always known it. Deford even reserved a special enthusiasm for "the teams that don't even have a whole state," e.g. University of Northern Iowa, the "littler brother" in Iowa State and the University of Iowa's sibling rivalry.

Yet this pattern was not inevitable. Some states created university systems like that advocated by President Hancher. Deford listed a few exceptions to his basic rule, as well, in which the State University is actually the more prominent and prestigious "flagship." Though not mentioned by Deford, Iowa is technically one of those exceptions.

This may come as a surprise to others, and it certainly surprised me. Iowa's oldest State University has never been found in Iowa State's home of Ames, but in Iowa City where it remains. The headlines of Hancher's and Hilton's day constantly referred to "SUI," for *State University of Iowa*. Since then, Iowa has informally adopted the usage common to other states, yet State University of Iowa still exists in Iowa law and other formal documents. By itself this is arguably more factoid than fact, and readily ceded to the trivia buffs. But it is connected to bigger events and issues, and illustrates how large features of history can be the easiest to forget: when they extend beyond single turning points, things often become a background to day-to-day life, and their absence from the record is little noted because their presence was little noted.

INTRODUCTION

Much the same phenomenon applies to people. A president of the United States can serve only one term and remain a public figure long after; a popular artist can produce a one-hit wonder and still have some currency in old age. By contrast, public officials like university presidents can occupy a prominent office for decades, appear frequently in the news and leave lasting influences, only to become nearly unknown within a couple of generations.

On this score, both Presidents Hilton and Hancher are notable, partial exceptions. While their accomplishments and the battles they fought, and perhaps even their existence as persons, are nearly forgotten, their names have shared a curious ability not just to survive but to prosper. The coliseum named in honor of Hilton's efforts to see it and a larger cultural center built has long been familiar to Iowa State alumni. In recent years Iowa State basketball's "Hilton Magic" has carried the name toward national recognition. The prominence of Hancher's name, if narrower geographically, is no less deep. Growing up in eastern Iowa I knew of Hancher Auditorium from childhood, long before I had heard of either president or given any thought to a college choice.

That the names of Hilton and Hancher have survived, in some sense together, offers one reason to reexamine both of them. It is by no means the only one. They fought a series of political duels with one another, with results of great potential interest today, as Iowa State has leapt past the University of Iowa as the state's largest school. The 2015 controversy over a revised budget formula that would have awarded Iowa State (and cost the University of Iowa) proportionately was a very faint echo of the Hancher-Hilton clashes, but presents further grounds to recall them as context.

Additionally, James Hilton and Virgil Hancher were both interesting persons, whose eventful lives serve as valuable context for one another. Each was born to a rural household at the end of the 19th century, and took parallel routes through subsequent decades' upheavals to leadership roles in a space-age society. Inevitably, their stories are rich beyond just their conflict with each other. Hilton's early life approaches an American answer to Dickens, while as president he found himself entangled with events as disparate as panty raids and pranking Nikita Kruschev. President Hancher found himself embattled long before Hilton's presidency, conciliating an offended Grant Wood his first year in office, and fending off legislative witch-hunts more than once thereafter. He may also be the only college president to suffer a literal heart attack during a football game, and stay through the end anyway.

The core of *Hancher vs. Hilton* is, nonetheless, their arguments. Interpreting these involves some difficulty, as they were often complex and only resolved in a practical sense. Among other authors to review the same issues, the passage of time has produced no more than a partial consensus. *A History of the University of Iowa in the 20th Century* asserts bluntly that Hancher "hated" James Hilton[6]; writing in *A Sesquicentennial History of Iowa State University*, David Hamilton concurs that the two presidents "detested one another."[7] Yet their conclusions about which institution typically received less public money than it deserved, and which received more, are exactly opposite. Each

INTRODUCTION

author predictably finds that his subject was the one shorted in favor of the other's.

If nothing else, I believe this offers a useful answer to any readers who may protest that the University of Iowa does not really have a rivalry with ISU, and that only Iowa State regards their contests as somehow special. Even if the indifference claimed by many Iowa fans toward sporting rivalry is granted, for argument's sake, the universities remain rivals at another more fundamental level. Where the prize of public support is concerned neither one can feign indifference for long.

Writing about one part of this ongoing contest thus offers an opportunity and a challenge. I hope that the stories to follow will interest devotees of both schools, and partly for this reason, I would like to be as fair as possible. I have attempted to withhold most judgments until the end. Otherwise my intent has been an interested neutrality—yet no narrator is ever truly neutral, and I am certainly not.

Raised just a few dozen miles from Iowa City, I will confess to sporting an Iowa Hawkeyes jacket for parts of my childhood. Into adolescence, however, I displayed no genuine interest in collegiate or other athletics. By the time I was old enough to consider more immediate college allegiances, I had determined to study graphic design; as the University of Iowa does not offer this as a major it was never in the running. Ultimately enrolling at Iowa State, like many teenaged misfits I embraced the college community which proved much more congenial than high school. I cheered enthusiastically for ISU, and possibly booed the University of Iowa even more enthusiastically. While 16 years have passed since graduation day and I live several hundred miles away, I still have a closet half-filled with ISU apparel. If my enthusiasm for sports is reduced, in adulthood, I retain a dependable pleasure at seeing the Iowa Hawkeyes defeated regardless of their opponent. In all candor, though no longer proud of this fact, the corners of my mouth still turn up reflexively even at embarrassments for the University of Iowa entirely unrelated to athletics.

Despite all this I entertain some hope of being fair. Reflexes aside, I cannot as an adult sustain any real negative opinion of the University of Iowa (even if its teams are a separate matter). Nor for that matter am I unwilling to acknowledge faults at Iowa State. If I am tempted to smugness at, e.g., some report of the U of I receiving high marks as a "party school," the temptation passes quickly when I consider Iowa State students' sustained campaign to eliminate the annual VEISHEA festival by starting small but utterly reasonless riots every few years. Further, like Mr. Deford Cyclone fans have traditionally savored cheering for an underdog, but in the battles between Hilton and Hancher the favorite can be difficult to pin down. Hilton's administration played hardball more than once, and while State University of Iowa enjoyed its share of victories, most were a long time in coming.

Last but not least, I believe that I can relate President Hancher's side of an argument fairly because I have come to sympathize with him in many ways. This may have been the greatest surprise in the course of my research, frankly. The portrait of Virgil Hancher that emerges from Iowa State's version of history is one of a villainous, almost fanatical determination to hold back the school's advancement. As I read more deeply into events, however, I discovered a thoughtful, wide-ranging intellect, whose arguments are fascinating and often challeng-

INTRODUCTION

ing even if I find their conclusions unconvincing. I have great admiration for President Hilton also, and of the two I suspect that I would enjoy meeting him more. But I feel a stronger empathy with Hancher, with the types of battles he fought, and the way he fought them.

I cannot pretend that I regret missing out on attending a University of Iowa at Ames. But if I don't believe the alternative has been a mistake, I'm not certain that Hancher's arguments were entirely wrong, either. I respect him for making them, even as I respect Hilton for his opposition.

I hope to do justice to both.

LOCATIONS

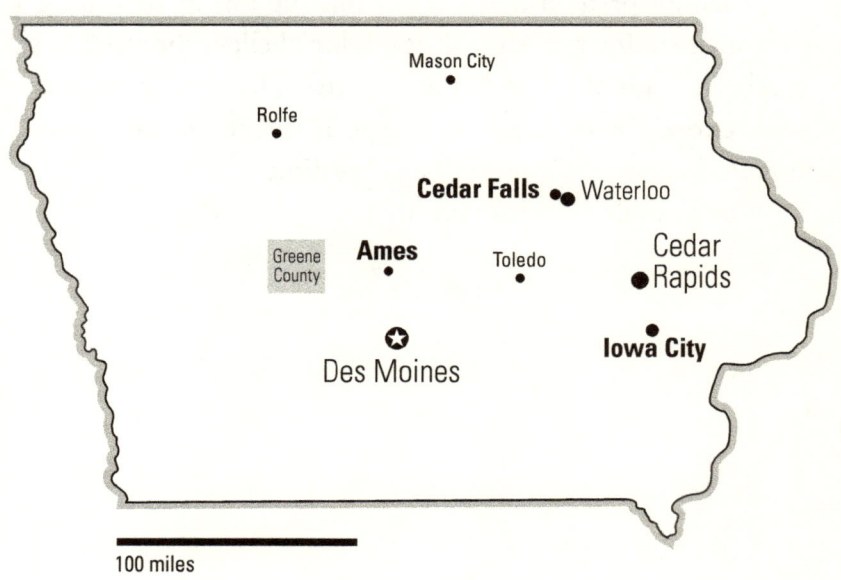

A NOTE ON NAMES

Confusion over names is a minor but persistent point of contention in *Hancher vs. Hilton*. If practical use never became entirely as muddled as some feared, the surfeit of names does complicate any retrospective of the whole era. Within a single decade, Iowa's three public colleges went through seven names in addition to assorted nicknames and abbreviations. The following summary therefore seems justified.

State University of Iowa (SUI) did not consistently adopt "University of Iowa" for day-to-day use until after President Hancher left office in 1964. The shorter name nonetheless appeared before then at times, as did many references simply to "the University" until Iowa State changed its name. As SUI has since fallen out of use and "U of I" might refer to other institutions in certain contexts, "Iowa" is now often used as a shorthand. (In light of many references to the identical name of the entire state, I have nonetheless tried to minimize this.) The University of Iowa is located in Iowa City and its athletes are the Hawkeyes.

Iowa State University (ISU) was still Iowa State College (ISC) when James Hilton took office in 1953, implementing its current name during his presidency. The shorter "Iowa State" has received widespread use before and since. Iowa State is located in Ames and its athletes are the Cyclones.

Iowa State Teachers College (ISTC) briefly became State College of Iowa (SCI) in 1961, before settling on its current name, University of Northern Iowa (UNI), in 1967. Under all three names it has remained in Cedar Falls, and its athletes are the Panthers.

Iowa's State Board of Education assumed oversight of Iowa's public colleges (and smaller specialized institutions) in 1909. In 1955, it became the Iowa Board of Regents.

CHAPTER ONE
The Scholar

Sympathy **is an** unlikely reaction to the life of Virgil Hancher, at first glance. Most of Hancher's life seems like a steady rise through privilege and rank, eventually delivering him to the presidency of a major university before he was 45 years old. I have a hunch, too, that the modern University of Iowa might be not only unsympathetic but outright repelled if confronted anew with Hancher's appointment as president. A Chicago corporate lawyer, lacking any professional academic experience beyond a single course taught while a graduate student, Hancher's career highlights included counseling General Motors executives on defeating antitrust charges.[1] His most ardent supporter on the Board of Education, an old fraternity brother[2], forgot to mention until after the board made its decision that Hancher was being sued for stock fraud. That this unconventional new president was eager to try out his theories on educational reform would not, I believe, do much to convert doubters.[3]

If this résumé was not quite so great an encumbrance in 1940 as it might be today, winning over his many constituencies was a tall order for Hancher all the same. What was more it may have been, in some sense, the first real challenge of his life. Without cheapening the work Hancher performed as either a student or a professional, his early life leaves the inescapable impression of a golden boy.

Born September 4, 1896 near the village of Rolfe, Iowa, Virgil Melvin Hancher grew up in a rural culture. But the Hancher family was some way from being deprived, particularly in comparison with that of its only child's future rival. In North Carolina the Hiltons were putting food on the table and a roof over their children's heads, but not much more. Melvin Park Hancher was by contrast "one of Iowa's best-known breeders of blooded livestock."[4] A third cousin, Dr. John W. Hancher, served as president of Iowa Wesleyan University during the first several years of the new century.[5]

Virgil Hancher left no comprehensive record of his childhood, which I assume included its allotment of life's ordinary defeats and disappointments. The memories which he and friends did record nonetheless reinforce a sense of someone generally in fortune's favor. Recalling his difficult beginnings at State University of Iowa, the most vivid episode Hancher offers is an all-night delay during his first journey to Iowa City, when storms washed out the train tracks. "The needed reconstruction took most of the night. As a result, we arrived in Iowa City 12 hours later—at 8 o'clock in the morning—unshaven, tired and hungry, and without anyone at the station to greet us."[6]

THE SCHOLAR

Significantly, loneliness is the only specific dissatisfaction throughout Hancher's reminiscences of his freshman year. Though he points to structural reasons, in an era before formal orientation or a student union or even school dormitories, his memories of isolation might reveal more about the student than about his college. During the same freshman year that Hancher describes as lonely and unhappy, one of "the few loyal friends" he found seems to have regarded his acquaintance with Virgil Hancher as nearly a full social circle by itself; fellow freshman Earl Hall was already embarked on a lifetime of championing Hancher's infinite merits. Despite which, the university's future president seriously considered transferring to Northwestern. Though allowing some thought for friends like Hall, Hancher suggests that he might have abandoned State University of Iowa but for his father, "who was a stubborn man…"

Even amid his doubt and despondence, it never seems to have been in question that Hancher was going to attend college somewhere, and graduate. Accounts of his life don't mention want of funds ever being a concern; want of talent certainly wasn't one. After his freshman year, the star of Rolfe High School had little difficulty making a name for himself again in a larger arena.

His new friend Hall knew of Hancher while still living two counties away in western Iowa, before fate introduced them personally in Iowa City. Reading news of "a Rolfe high schooler who was really burning up the league in forensics," Hall was already impressed. As friend and classmate at college, his admiration for Hancher only deepened. Hall later summarized the undergraduate Virgil Hancher as "the all-time-All-American in extracurricular affairs," a brilliant speaker and obviously bound for high office.[7] If Hall's breathless enthusiasm for his friend was an outlier, his respect was not. When Hancher completed his Bachelor of Arts in 1918 he was not only the top scholar in his class, but its president. After four years the "frightened freshman from a little country town"[8] had become a confident young adult with brilliant prospects, esteemed by his peers.

Hancher seems to have felt a deep gratitude to the university, in response. Through the years and decades that followed, ability and ambition led him to bigger and brighter stages, yet his person and his thoughts often turned back toward Iowa. Graduating during America's engagement in World War I, Hancher served for a year in the U.S. Naval Reserve in Chicago. He then attended Oxford as a Rhodes Scholar, completing a second Bachelor of Arts at Worcester College in 1922. Yet he spent part of the same period back in Iowa, as summer help in a Mason City law firm and house guest of his friend Hall, who had begun his own career as a newsman. Hancher returned to their mutual alma mater to earn a Doctor of Jurisprudence in 1924, teaching one class for an absent professor. He qualified for the Iowa bar the same year.

Over the next few years Hancher continued his ambitious grand tour, and slowly began "returning home" to Chicago more than to Iowa. While planning another degree at Oxford, he spent part of 1926 in the Washington office of Chicago-based attorneys Butler, Lamb, Foster and Pope. Upon complet-

THE SCHOLAR

ing a Master of Arts degree in 1927, Hancher joined the firm's main office on LaSalle Street in downtown Chicago. In 1928 Hancher renewed his ties to northwest Iowa, marrying his fiancée Susan Cannon of Paullina, but the Hanchers began their own family in Evanston. (The new Mrs. Hancher was a 1924 graduate of the city's local university, coincidentally the same Northwestern to which her husband had considered transferring.) For the next dozen years Virgil Hancher practiced law on LaSalle Street, rising through the ranks of his employer as he had everywhere else. When the firm reorganized as Pope & Ballard in 1936, Hancher became a partner and took over responsibility for running the office. His efforts for clients, meanwhile, met with equal respect; his reorganization of the Chicago and Eastern Illinois Railroad under new bankruptcy laws served as a model for similar cases that followed.[9]

Still SUI did not leave Hancher's thoughts. He kept active in the University Club of Chicago. He helped raise money to build the student union which, as a freshman, he had felt the school sorely needed. He even served a term as president of the alumni association. Hancher was tempted by larger roles, too. Having spent most of a decade within higher education, in two very different forms, the institution itself fascinated him beyond his love for State University of Iowa. He had considered various academic posts over the years, and meanwhile Earl Hall's flattering talk of the SUI presidency stopped being completely fanciful upon Hall's appointment to the Iowa Board of Education. By early 1940 the board was deadlocked in the choice of a successor for outgoing President Gilmore, and had with much encouragement from Hall approached Hancher for serious discussions. Hancher demurred, however, still uncertain.[10] He had a home in Chicago, a young family, and a successful career. Less happily, he also had one or two troubling intrusions on what had until then been nearly a charmed life.

Virgil Hancher's life can reasonably be divided into two phases, at least for biographical purposes: before accepting the presidency of State University of Iowa, and after. Hancher spent nearly the rest of his life as SUI president, and those years encompass all of his significant legacies to history; from this perspective the 44 years before were all one extended prologue. Assuming the leadership of his alma mater marks a division between a private life and a public life. It also marks a division between a generally happy and successful life, and a life of more purpose, perhaps, but also of more frustration and loss.

No more than part of that last transition can be ascribed to coincidence. That portion, though, likely included the most painful. During the Hanchers' first decade of marriage, Mrs. Hancher gave birth to three children: Virgil, Jr. in 1931; Mary Susan in 1934; and Priscilla in 1938. As the Iowa Board of Education made a second, successful approach to Dr. Hancher in late August 1940, the youngest Hancher was severely ill with leukemia. Today the success rate for treating childhood leukemia is mercifully high. In 1940 it was near zero. Amid the sad, helpless time that must have resulted, it may be that the renewed approach by Hall and others seemed more compelling than before. The job interested Hancher already. Now, it also suggested a means for him and his family to move on from the looming loss.

THE SCHOLAR

Whatever his personal deliberations, Hancher accepted. A small, handwritten card provides at least some impression of his thoughts. Writing to SUI College of Education Dean Paul Packer, Hancher expressed relief and a hope, at least, for recovery: "Now that the decision has been made, I am looking forward with great enthusiasm to the new field. Happily the decision has had a tonic effect upon my wife. ... My ambitions now are in the University and its welfare is my first concern. May the days ahead be fruitful ones."[11] Enacting the decision waited only on his youngest daughter's health. Hancher and family delayed moving, to grant "adorable little Priscilla" as peaceful an end to her brief life as possible. By October, however, SUI's new president was prepared to join the November 1, 1940 Homecoming and begin a new phase in life with a clean slate.

As it transpired, events denied him any such opportunity.

Even before Hancher accepted it, his presidency was hobbled, being in essence an unhappy compromise between rival candidates within the university. Reluctant to select either Packer or Graduate Dean George Stoddard, and thereby embitter the passionate advocates for each, the Board of Education divided up disappointment evenly by pursuing Hancher. While board president George Baker offered appropriate praise in newspaper announcements, a *Cedar Rapids Gazette* item a few days before had reported Baker and Packer as leading voices in a faction that "contended Hancher not qualified by scholarship, educational or administrative experience."[12] It was difficult to rebut this criticism, furthermore. Two years later Hancher himself dismissed his brief teaching experience as not worth mentioning.[13] This formal distance from the academic profession would dog Hancher's efforts as a university leader, long after he made up for it in practice.[14]

Meanwhile another member of the Board of Education proposed to forestall Hancher's reconciliation with academia before it began. He, too, had cause for his criticism, expressed even more forcefully than Baker et al. Under a blaring headline "Would Rescind Hancher Election," the October 21 *Gazette* reported that board member Thomas W. Keenan regretted his vote for Hancher, and urged his colleagues to overturn the choice. Keenan said that he had learned just days before, long after the board voted, that "Hancher is one of several defendants in a suit for the recovery of $110,000 and charging fraud and conspiracy by the Victory Corporation, Chicago, its officers, directors and several stockholders."[15]

The Victory Corporation fiasco's full details are, after several decades, obscured by distance and complexity. That same complexity nonetheless contributes to its larger significance: it looks like a swindle of some sort, whatever its legal technicalities. In 1928, Hancher and various business associates had joined Pope & Ballard partner James J. Forstall in organizing Victory Corporation, to invest in stocks and bonds. The name alone almost reeks of smart young men too confident in their cleverness, as the great market crash the following year proved that they were. Before the bubble burst, many of the investors provided promissory notes for their Victory Co. stock. Hancher purchased his own shares with $2,000 worth of notes. When the market crashed, Forstall declined to pursue payment on such IOUs, but Hancher determined to make good on his obligation at least in part and his mother purchased the notes for $1,000.[16] Several years later, disgruntled shareholder Thomas

Tighe claimed that this sale along with the nonpayment of other notes amounted to fraud. Tighe then filed a six-figure lawsuit against Hancher, alongside Victory Co. generally.

I confess to throwing up my hands at re-trying *Tighe v. Hancher*. In my defense I suspect that the surviving records are inadequate even for an expert. One of Hancher's former colleagues sent an earnest defense of him to the SUI Alumni Association, though part of it rests on a plea that *it was the 1920s, all of us lost our reason in those years*.[17] In court, after brief initial sparring the proceedings ended in early 1941 with a stipulation, a less formal settlement in which all of the details remain private.[18] Prior to this resolution, of course, Thomas Keenan directed his complaints as much toward the board's late appraisal of the lawsuit as toward the suit's merit. His colleague Earl Hall, who stage-managed every step of the board's decision, had been in frequent contact with Hancher going back to their college days. Hall knew of the lawsuit but "forgot" to mention it until after a public announcement of Hancher's appointment—an announcement which the newsman Hall, overcome with pride in his old friend, made himself without first consulting the board's president.[19] Possibly the events surrounding Victory Corporation and *Tighe v. Hancher* still lack solid evidence of any purposeful deceit, but in that event they must be acknowledged as lacking evidence of any consistent good judgment.

If Virgil Hancher's integrity is to be judged on appearance, however, any ruling should take into account the long term. Hancher served as president for many years, and received criticism in that office many times. Yet criticism of Hancher on ethical grounds is practically nonexistent. After the other board members all stood by his election[20], the threatened scandal of *Tighe v. Hancher* evaporated, never reappearing even when other critics were at their most belligerent. Hancher went on from a compromised beginning to earn confidence and respect at national levels, and eventually local esteem followed. It was simply rarely, if ever, easy.

Beginning his administration in the last months of 1940, President Hancher was again joining State University of Iowa as world war threatened. America's entry into the conflict scarcely one year later swiftly redefined Hancher's first several years in office. His plans for a proper library, for reorganizing the school's administration, for more deeply rethinking higher education itself, all went on hold as he performed triage responses to rapidly fluctuating enrollment and worked out where to house 2,000 navy cadets. Looking back afterward, Hancher characterized the entire decade as "stabilized abnormality,"[21] and described the 13 months before Pearl Harbor as the only normal year he experienced.

Even a "normal" year as SUI's president included headaches. Upon taking office, Hancher inherited at least two embarrassing messes. The athletics department was several thousand dollars in debt, and had been in default on the interest for Iowa Stadium (today's Kinnick) since 1937.[22] One frustrated bondholder actually tried to foreclose on the stadium.[23] Recent financially successful seasons for the Hawkeyes permitted making up the arrears, fortunately, within weeks of Hancher's inauguration, but paying down the larger debt took a full decade.[24]

THE SCHOLAR

Virgil M. Hancher, early in his presidency of State University of Iowa.
F.W. Kent Collection, University Archives, The University of Iowa Libraries.

HANCHER VS. HILTON

Sorting out strained relations with Grant Wood proved a years-long process also. Since 1935 the creator of *American Gothic* had been part of SUI's art department. Much of the department cared little for Wood or his regionalist art, however.[25] In late 1940 *Time* published a story exposing the tensions. New president Hancher had small enthusiasm for the artist, himself, but made efforts to prevent a complete rupture. He persuaded Wood to delay any decision about leaving until the appointment of a new dean of liberal arts, and then found one capable of keeping the artist, if not happy, then at least in the department until his death from cancer in 1942.[26]

The postwar 1940s brought still more controversies, although one at least ended in a major success. A Medical Service Plan which Hancher introduced in 1947 remains in use nearly 70 years later, and other colleges have adopted it as a model.[27] Yet the plan, like many reforms to the recompense of health services, initially faced fierce opposition. An Iowa Medical Society committee declared the plan not only "the hottest topic in the state" but "communistic;" an SUI professor went to the press warning against it[28]; and one department head quit the College of Medicine in protest.

For Hancher all of this was more than balanced by the broader approval which greeted the plan—and by the broader disapproval which it prevented. Under old rules, the college's part-time department heads could combine their university salaries with potentially unlimited income from private medical practice. All the rest of the medical faculty had to relinquish their practice fees to a common "fee fund" and get by on salaries alone. As a result, a vast gap had opened between the bosses and everyone else. Combined with concerns about tenure and an overemphasis on private practice at the expense of teaching, much of the college was ready to revolt. According to Hancher, five doctors had already quit and another 10 were open about plans to depart, absent some new arrangement.[29]

The new arrangement included a revised salary progression, and a sliding scale for how much additional money faculty could pocket for work in private practice. Departments would collect all private practice fees for its faculty in a common pool, then make payments in proportion to each doctor's position on the scale up to his allotted maximum. Hancher was at pains to deny that all this represented socialism. "Presumably the university has a right to put every man in the college of medicine on a salary—just as the University of Chicago does," he argued. "If it has that right, then it seems to me that surely it can do a lesser thing. It can set a limit on their salaries."[30]

In the event, most of the College of Medicine found the system satisfactory whatever its economic philosophy, and faculty felt proud of it as largely their own work.[31] Certainly Hancher had not personally designed the system. But as president he had made the judgment to support its implementation, in the face of resistance, and time has vindicated this as an instance of valuable leadership. Multiple assessments have echoed that of Dean Robert Hardin that at SUI "the plan saved the Medical College."[32]

The university's medical programs were the major realizations of Hancher's early hope for fruitful days, through his first decade in office. A year after launching the Medical Service Plan, SUI opened the Iowa hospital school for severely handicapped children. Though a small program limited to a maximum 20 children, the small scale was intentional, focusing on outlier cases whose disabilities placed them beyond the capabilities of any of the state's other agencies.[33] In the years that followed, Hancher approved changes to the school of nursing to create a first-class, regionally significant program. In 1949 the school became SUI's 10th full college[34], adding a graduate program two years later. All of this deserved and received commendation. Beyond the departments of medicine, however, the same period was a bleak one.

For all the great battles with Iowa State and its president that lay ahead, and the many disappointments that resulted, 1949 was the nadir of Virgil Hancher's career. A few years earlier, an issue of the university *News Bulletin* celebrating SUI's 100th anniversary had jauntily captioned a photo "Virgil M. Hancher: Confident of University's Future."[35] America had emerged victorious from war, and enrollments were rapidly rebounding. Hancher was gradually reorganizing a presidency that managed 32 direct reports when he first took office[36], and might have found time at last to concentrate on deeper issues within SUI and higher education. Instead, he spent much of his ninth year under siege.

For many other states the late 1940s brought a postwar boom to higher education, both in enrollment and in funding. Iowa, Hancher commented in later years, "held back."[37] Newly elected Governor William Beardsley led Iowa's fiscal reticence. In a period when state funds formed a much larger share of university budgets than today, including in Iowa, Beardsley aspired to cut the state's contribution to one-fourth of colleges' expenses.[38] When the schools' advocates protested that Iowa

THE SCHOLAR

was prospering, Beardsley insisted that appropriations could not be made "on the assumption" that revenues would continue at present levels.[39] So determined was the governor to battle excess in higher education budgets that he dispatched auditors to seek it out. Unfortunately for President Hancher, at SUI they found something.

The auditors found an available balance of $1,912,000 in the State University of Iowa treasury, hundreds of thousands of dollars greater than SUI had reported when making its request for state appropriations.[40] The Hancher administration could and did offer simple, straightforward reasons for the discrepancy. Both enrollment and the price of many supplies had fluctuated significantly in recent years. Upward pressure on faculty salaries had been more steady, but as a result the university had been unable to replace many of those who left mid-year, leaving some of the money budgeted for salaries unspent.[41] By every reasonable measure the university's accounting was entirely above-board, and no one charged SUI with intentionally concealing the surplus.[42] But these facts were, to some extent, beside the point. Politicians had sought a pretext for hostilities, and having found one they felt entitled to commence blasting.

Members of Iowa's House of Representatives unleashed a barrage of stockpiled grievances. Kingsley M. Clarke of Adel, a dissatisfied SUI alumnus, reveled in mocking a committee's recent praise of the school as "the best in the nation." Clarke vented anger at the medical college, the law school, undergraduate education and the entire institution. The university, Rep. Clarke thundered, simply "threw a mass of facts" at undergrads and called it education. It served no real function beyond providing a "license to work" in the form of a degree.[43] Lawrence

Putney of Gladbrook extended Clarke's swipe at the College of Medicine, denouncing its limited admissions. "This medical school down there needs some investigation and I don't mean maybe," Putney said. "They've built the restrictions so high that you almost have to have a grandfather who came over in the Mayflower to get in."[44]

Not only Clarke but a majority of the House agreed with Putney's call for investigations. Rep. Clarke introduced an amendment to the Board of Education appropriations, already approved by the Senate, authorizing investigation of SUI salaries and teaching practices. Another amendment addressed Putney's complaint. Many in Iowa had acknowledged a shortage of doctors for some time[45], and representatives called on SUI "to admit 120 freshman medical students or as nearly that many as possible before any of the money would become available."[46]

A few voices within the House dissented. Rep. Normon Norlond of Kensett accompanied his objections with a particularly interesting countermove; proposing that investigators target Iowa State College as well, he hoped to make the measure distasteful to ISC partisans and thereby derail the entire plan. Norlond's strategy failed, in the end, but resistance from the Senate proved more effective. A solid majority of senators refused to countenance the House's amended appropriations bill. Approaching the end of the legislature's biennial duties, a number of representatives chose to reverse their votes, remove the offending amendments, and go home. Before long, Clarke himself scrambled to retreat from most of his assertions.[47]

The outcome was far from a victory for Hancher and SUI nonetheless. The president had attended much of the appro-

THE SCHOLAR

priations debate in person, and put a brave face on things. At one point he suggested he would welcome an investigation, implying that legislators might learn a thing or two.[48] More often, though, he had no formal comment. Privately he and associates still referred to the most intense battering as "Bloody Thursday" decades later.[49]

The casualties were not entirely restricted to prestige, either. The total Board of Education budget finally approved by the General Assembly, though larger than Governor Beardsley's recommendation, was essentially equal to current costs, and school administrators had no doubt that many costs would be much greater through the two years ahead. Additionally, the SUI share (exclusive of university hospitals funding) was less than Iowa State College's by $50,000 per year. At the time, ISC enrollment was just more than two-thirds that of SUI. Newspapers noted that "The appropriations committee did not explain why the university's operating fund was less than Iowa State's," but most concurred that the audit findings played a role. Off the record, "several committee members said privately that the university had a larger free balance than had been anticipated."[50]

If all this were not enough, critics ensured in two other ways that the "warning" to SUI, the Board of Education and Hancher himself had its effect. Earl Hall had inevitably supported his friend throughout his trials, and denounced the governor's leadership in a newspaper editorial.[51] In the process Hall essentially dared the governor to deny him reappointment to the Board of Education, upon the end of his term; Governor Beardsley felt no hesitation accepting the dare. For their part legislators kept resentment over the audit results alive for years to come through a new committee. Under the Budget and Financial Control Committee, a budget examiner's office would "pre-audit" every expense at all of the state's public colleges. The Board of Education's president called it, frankly, "a piece of spite legislation designed to embarrass and harass the schools."[52]

Virgil Hancher certainly agreed. He emerged from these events feeling persecuted and discouraged, as well as embarrassed. Many of Hancher's subsequent remarks and deeds are characterized by a pessimism, subtle at times but never dispelled. A letter to his friend "Buster," known otherwise as state Senator J. Kendall Lynes, lay bare the SUI president's views one year after "Bloody Thursday." Hancher confessed that "I returned to Iowa in 1940 believing that the people of this state wanted a first class University, and other first class institutions as well. I still believe that this is what they want. After being here a decade, however, I am not quite as sure as I once was."[53]

Hancher's letter to Sen. Lynes, along with the experiences that prompted it, is helpful in understanding another letter that followed. Though written three years before James Hilton became Iowa State's president, Hancher's correspondence with Brown University President Henry M. Wriston is one of the most significant documents in the Hancher vs. Hilton conflict.

During much of his own presidency, Hancher was active in the Association of American Universities, holding at various points the offices of AAU secretary-treasurer, vice president and president.[54] A still-select group of major universities today, the AAU's membership was even more restrictive in 1950.

THE SCHOLAR

Extending its ranks was a topic of perennial debate. Wriston's suggestion to Hancher in July 1950, therefore, presumably seemed innocuous. Pointing to the growing stature of many land-grant colleges, Wriston proposed that "I think it would ease our political tensions a good deal and I think it would give us a good deal of strength... If, for example, [Indiana University President] Herman Wells would nominate Purdue and you would nominate Ames it would break a situation which, it seems to me, is over the years, going to cause us a great deal of difficulty." Curiously, Wriston emphasized that he left this to Hancher's discretion: "However, I am not going to make a nomination which would be repugnant to you."[55]

Wriston may only have been reluctant to tell a fellow university president how to handle affairs within his own state. Had he truly expected that Hancher would find the suggestion repugnant, he probably would not have offered it at all. But if Brown's president was simply being cautious his caution proved remarkably prescient. President Wells, Hancher responded, undoubtedly "would be exceedingly reluctant to propose Purdue for membership just as I am reluctant to propose Iowa State College, and for the same reasons." Declaring ignorance of the political tensions to which Wriston referred, Hancher was acutely sensitive to others:

> In each case it would give powerful weight to a movement to create two universities in each state. Perhaps California and Michigan and certain other states can afford that luxury, but Iowa cannot, and I doubt if Indiana could. If the land-grant institutions are recognized as universities, then we may expect that with their agricultural connection they will increase their

31

pressure on our legislatures with the prospect that the existing universities will suffer in relation to the land-grant colleges.[56]

Given Hancher's trials in the 18 months preceding this letter, his wariness of a zero-sum competition is understandable. State University of Iowa had obviously been slighted in favor of ISC in the 1949 appropriations. Rep. Norlond's attempt to deflect SUI critics also implied a belief that other legislators, partial to Iowa State, would consent to a legislative witch-hunt at State University of Iowa but respond differently if ISC were included. In this context, Hancher's declining to campaign actively on Iowa State's behalf seems no more than fair.

Yet the issue of whether Hancher's wariness was simply defensive concern for his own institution, or influenced by deeper disdain, is complicated by an odd digression that followed. A few weeks before Wriston's letter, another AAU-school president had also written Hancher supporting membership for Iowa State, proposing that "The recent organization of the work in atomic energy under Dr. Frank Spedding, it seems to me, has made it an institution of unusual significance."[57] Though Wriston made no mention of the program, which operates today as Ames Lab, Hancher included a rebuttal to its merits amid their correspondence. Asserting that Spedding appeared to consult with Iowa State's President Charles Friley only to the extent of announcing decisions for Friley to confirm, Hancher questioned "to what extent does the College control the Institute and to what extent does the Institute control the College?" Implying strongly that this made Iowa State suspect as an educational institution, Hancher asked "Would

THE SCHOLAR

the Association of American Universities be prepared to consider Brookhaven [National Laboratory] for membership?"[58]

At one time or another everyone "thinks out loud," and Virgil Hancher was no exception. A colleague's handwritten comment on an invitation to the University of Florida centennial, preserved among his papers, once offered "President Hancher Perhaps I should go to see that you don't say anything you shouldn't!" Below it, the president responded: "Probably I'd say it anyway! (V.H.)"[59] A few months after his letter to Wriston, Hancher apparently decided he had done exactly that. In a letter to the University of Missouri's president, carbon-copied to Wriston, Hancher began: "In order that my position may be somewhat clearer with respect to land grant colleges, I would like to add a footnote to the discussion…" Signing up some of these schools would make the AAU's membership more representative, he declared, and might thereby enhance its authority on education issues. Therefore, Hancher continued, "I would be quite willing to have the Association select the ten best land-grant colleges in the U.S. and add them to the membership, and I would expect to see and would be delighted to see Iowa State and Purdue among the ten."[60]

In combination all of this is puzzling, off-the-cuff or no. It seems fair to place at least as much weight on Hancher's revised letter, as the product of genuine second thoughts, as on the earlier letter; the incongruous musing on Ames Lab might be evidence of a letter dashed off carelessly rather than of deep hostility. Meanwhile, much of Hancher's other correspondence is consistently reticent about any expansion of the AAU at all. To whatever extent he may have remained privately opposed to membership for Iowa State, it was by no means unique in that regard.

Yet there are hints that Hancher's scorn for the Friley administration was more than a single, random complaint. A decade earlier, Friley had convinced the Board of Education to abandon a pension proposal which Hancher later worked to revive.[61] Writing to the board's president in 1948, he paid Friley a backhanded compliment for success in obtaining what Hancher felt was much more generous funding than SUI received.[62] Hancher also suggested that federal support of Ames Lab would give a further boost to ISC's budget, and that as a result State University of Iowa's needs should have higher priority in state appropriations. Taken all together, it's clear that Hancher was frustrated by budgetary reticence—and growing resentful of what he perceived as favoritism toward Iowa State—even before the fiascoes of 1949.

In light of more direct attempts to check Iowa State ambitions, which follow, it's tempting to perceive a bias on Hancher's part, firmly in place already and only concealed for a time behind politeness or philosophical differences. Without veering too early into such judgments, for now I will merely note a degree of doubt toward this interpretation. If Hancher perceived a zero-sum game in higher education, his desire was not necessarily to triumph at Iowa State's expense but to find a more equitable approach.

In the decade ahead, he argued repeatedly that Iowa's land-grant college and its university ought to complement one another, rather than compete. So long as other institutions were content to pursue their distinct roles while SUI pursued its own, happier coexistence may still have seemed within reach.

THE SCHOLAR

If Hancher held out less hope for better relations with President Friley, that did not necessarily color his attitude toward Iowa State as a whole. Friley was stepping down in 1953. A great deal would depend on what kind of person replaced him.

CHAPTER TWO

The Salesman

When James G. Hilton recalled of his late father, and Iowa State's 10th president, that "he lived on top of a hog barn"[1] I wrote down the phrase without response. It was simply too colorful not to record. It did not occur to me that it might be literal truth; an exaggeration of some less outlandish episode, possibly, or a figurative use of language perhaps. Dr. Hilton had been speaking of a deep humility that characterized his father, and so his words presumably referred more to the type of person James H. Hilton had been, than to exact details of any home he once occupied. They had to.

I have reversed that opinion since, for two reasons. The first is a forthright statement in a sketch biography which President Hilton authored after his retirement: describing one makeshift housing solution while a freshman at North Carolina State College, he explains "This time I moved to the college hog barn and got a job milking 15 to 20 cows daily for my room and board. The hogs had the downstairs portion of the structure, and a fellow student named Carl Tatum and I occupied the upstairs apartment."[2] The second reason is that Hilton describes endless such episodes from his early life, always in the most prosaic, uninflected language. Immediately after noting a hog barn as his residence, Hilton relates once slipping on its steps and tearing his only decent pants. "Completely out of money at the time, I did not see how I could buy another pair, so I just sat down on the steps and cried," he writes. This is what happened at the time, and what he did in response, and that's all; the adult Hilton neither displays nor asks pity for the predicaments of his youth.

Hilton's ultimate, quiet verdict on his life always seems to emphasize good fortune rather than misfortune. As he allows, he did not always see it that way while living it. That's perfectly easy to understand. If James Hilton and Virgil Hancher began life in roughly similar circumstances, from a larger perspective, and eventually met in equivalent elevated roles, their routes in between diverged widely. For Hilton, advancement was less an escalator than one crumbling, humbling hog barn stair after another.

The household into which James Harold Hilton was born November 20, 1899, was not distinguished for better or for worse. The Hilton farm was an ordinary, small family farm in its time and place, its place being western North Carolina, nine miles from Hickory. Henry M. Hilton grew whatever crops would grow, and occasionally worked in a sawmill. James and four siblings that followed helped their parents with the endless labor of pre-mechanized agriculture, and if the surplus was consistently modest, bills were at least paid and mouths fed. The eldest Hilton child probably wouldn't have struck anyone as positioned for great things at the time, or for years after. Despite which, he too just might have credited all of the achievements that followed to a stubborn parent's push.

Unlike the Hanchers, Hilton's parents could provide him neither money nor connection nor even model. His father had an eighth-grade education, and of his mother he could only write later that she "attended" the college of Weaverville for a time.[3] Alice Clampitt Hilton nonetheless determined that her children receive an education. She had been a teacher for several years, before her marriage, and perhaps also desired that her son complete the path she had been able to start but not finish. Whatever her reason, Mrs. Hilton insisted that James go to college.[4]

This was a powerful commandment given that merely completing high school proved far from automatic. Rural North Carolina had public high schools by Hilton's adolescence, but not so many that he could attend one while living at home. Instead he boarded at Startown Farm Life School, as did many of his classmates. Farm life schools emphasized agriculture, while offering some broader curricula and shoestring-budget extracurricular activities. While Hilton took advantage of the opportunities, most of his academic career was one of steady plodding; in his own words he "was no more than an average student."[5] He participated in debating contests, but won no particular reputation among his classmates, let alone two counties away.

Hilton's chief obstacle as a student was, however, simply money. The need for funds distracted him from his studies again and again, beginning as early as Startown School. Enrollment at the school was free but room and board were not. Hilton worked part-time on the school farm, and his family sent payments of produce from their own fields, but by his junior year Hilton was looking hard for economies. He set up housekeeping with another student, saving on their room and board at the cost of living off their own wretched cooking. The following summer Hilton went through three jobs looking for something to last even those few months. Fighting with a hostile coworker cost his job at a furniture factory. Next obtaining work as a taxi driver, but without any experience driving, he concluded swiftly that this work was not meant for him either. Finally, Hilton found agreeable employment with a wholesale grocer.

In return Hilton's efforts found favor with his new employer, Mr. Riddle, who provided a second enjoinder to become educated. It was needed; the recent dismal experience as his own cook had convinced Hilton to postpone his return to school until he could save enough to afford decent meals. Mr. Riddle would not hear of it. Somehow he perceived promise in his employee and insisted he return to Startown, pledging financial assistance and even calling the school himself to assure them that James Hilton would attend fall classes. Hilton could hardly help being impressed, and enrolled for his senior year determined once more to graduate.

His good intentions proved to be short-lived. Despite the powerful encouragement of Mr. Riddle along with whatever assistance he lent, Hilton was penniless again within two months. His final summary of his time at Startown Farm Life School is blunt: "I never quite finished."[6]

THE SALESMAN

Given James Hilton's eventual career, abandoning high school obviously did not mean abandoning education for good, for all that it might easily have done so. His mother's admonishment may deserve some credit, as might that of Mr. Riddle even if Hilton let him down for the time being. A good deal of credit must be awarded, also, to the First World War.

Like Virgil Hancher, Hilton was blessedly unscathed by the war that consumed many of their peers. In Hilton's case, he was still too young to serve when the United States joined the war, and in no hurry to enlist by lying about his age, particularly when America's mobilization soon presented more appealing opportunities. Like many colleges, North Carolina State was rapidly attenuated of able-bodied young men. Its dairy farm was so shorthanded that word reached Hilton all the way on the other side of the state, and Hilton answered. Before long he decamped from Startown and was, at 17, managing the college's dairy herd and effectively its entire farm.

The job was demanding, independent of age or experience. When summer arrived Hilton promptly hired his younger brother Clayton; together they still worked 15-hour days to keep the keep the farm going by themselves. The rewards were immense, however. Hilton declared the labor itself "a wonderful experience because we learned how to get a job done." On top of that, wartime conditions at North Carolina State soon presented an opportunity not merely to resume his studies where he left off, but to leap ahead. "In September," Hilton explained later, "my brother returned home to high school. I planned to return too, but since so many college age students were in military service, North Carolina State gave a number of us the opportunity to enter the freshman class even though we had not quite finished high school." Better still, "By entering in the fall of 1918 we were automatically part of the Student Army Training Corps (S.A.T.C.)," which meant a place in the college dormitories without fee.[7]

Such good fortune was transient, as ever. The war had spared Hilton to date, but the 1918 influenza epidemic did not. After a week in a crowded makeshift infirmary, Hilton was among those fortunate enough to leave alive if not healthy enough to do so unaided, and friends supported him the entire way back to his dorm. Within two days, he was back in the infirmary with pneumonia. Already ravaged by flu, he wrote afterward that "I guess I came about as close to dying as I have ever been."[8] Hilton survived, but by November he was out of the dormitories again, permanently. The war's end dissolved the SATC and with it the funding for his housing. Thus, by the spring of 1919, did James Hilton find himself quite literally living on top of a hog barn.

Somehow at least, he forever found a way to forestall disaster a bit longer. After crying in sheer despair when his fall from the barn steps tore a seam in his only respectable pants, Hilton found salvation in a farmhand's wife who repaired them. When summer arrived he found work building silos and sheep-dipping vats for the college's extension program, but once again with absolutely no experience in the core functions of the job. Somehow, though, "with the aid of good blueprints and some experienced construction help" he survived the season.[9]

THE SALESMAN

North Carolina State College must be credited with a profound transformation in James Hilton. He arrived as a high school dropout looking for work—despite Alice Hilton's and Mr. Riddle's personal entreaties to get a good education—and left as a college student seeking a better degree. That he left after just one year should not obscure this effect. In fact, Hilton was not entirely finished with North Carolina State. Nonetheless in the summer of 1919, he turned his eyes for the first time toward Iowa State College.

Hilton had resolved by this point on a firm direction for his studies. He would focus on animal husbandry, and while North Carolina State had offered plentiful hands-on experience, he wanted to be nearer the forefront of scientific agriculture. Examining college catalogs and surveying opinion around him, he narrowed his choices to two, then one. Hilton recounted later that he was settled on Cornell University in New York—until three acquaintances from his summer labor changed his mind.[10] Two graduates of Iowa State's animal husbandry program, R.S. Curtis and John Sloss, endorsed the program and offered help finding work in Ames. (Remarkably, both ambassadors share names with buildings at Iowa State, entirely by coincidence.) A third endorsement arrived along with the offer of a loan from B.W. Kilgore, Hilton's boss for the summer and the head of agricultural programs in North Carolina. If even he pointed to Iowa State, as far as Hilton was concerned, "That settled it!"[11]

Consensus indicated that Hilton was transferring to an institution of higher standards. What he found on arrival in Ames the next fall confirmed this, powerfully. Having left for Iowa State without waiting for its formal reply, Hilton only received it at the registrar's office: ISC had rejected his transfer application. The reasons were all too obvious in hindsight. Hilton's grades were mediocre, and North Carolina State was not accredited to the standard which ISC demanded. The awkward detail of not "quite" completing high school stood out as well. Imagining his reaction upon getting through the registration line, only to receive a copy of the letter rejecting his entire application, strikes me as a certain recurring pattern of nightmare made real; Hilton was, simply, stunned.

What happened next might almost have been fate itself, dropping all pretense of hidden workings. Hilton had already found board in Ames, with a Mrs. Mitchell. His landlady happened to be friends with a Miss Kelley, employed in the registrar's office. The obvious intervention resulted, and although 21st-century cynicism forces me to admit subtle forms of privilege are better documented than cosmic destiny, I readily understand that Hilton had no doubts: "…by noon I was registered as a sophomore. I will always feel a deep sense of gratitude to those people. In such small ways are entire lives changed."[12]

Hilton's gratitude toward Iowa State was indeed lasting, and deserved. Enrollment at Iowa State marked another great change in his life. Though he still had to balance studies with earning money to pay for them, from this point on he seems to have internalized the importance of an education. Nearly 21 years old, he no longer needed adults to steer him back toward a completed degree.

THE SALESMAN

By his enrollment at Iowa State College, Hilton may have been firmly rooted down to earth for life. His finances left nothing to chance, though, as he left the registrar with $25 to his name.[13] Certainly he no more anticipated he would ever become a college president than he can have known that Herman Knapp, the ISC registrar and soon Hilton's part-time employer, would as well in 1926. Even when cleaning President Pearson's own office, Hilton may have assumed that custodial work would be the only occasion he would occupy it as his job.

By the end of winter term, 1921, Hilton was in fact broke again and left school for several months as Jefferson County agent for the 4-H organization. He returned to Iowa State in the fall and made ends meet until the next summer. Then it was back to work, this time for the Iowa State extension service. Even as Virgil Hancher "traveled among the fountain-

James H. Hilton c. 1922.
University Photographs, Box 65, Iowa State University Library Special Collections.

heads of Europe's history"[14] on vacations from Oxford, Hilton spent his summer exploring back roads and rural communities throughout Iowa to study the impact of 4-H.

In late autumn 1922, Hilton completed a bachelor of science degree in animal husbandry. It was the first degree of his life, and would not be the last. Graduate opportunities beckoned, and that winter he returned to teach a short course in animal husbandry at Iowa State. Before completely immersing himself in graduate student life, however, he resolved on a break from the past several years' hand-to-mouth existence.

For the next three years Hilton resumed work with the Iowa State extension program, as its Greene County agent. Hilton and subsequent chroniclers highlight the experience as formative. Once more he was spending every day on the ground, meeting ordinary Iowans, listening to their concerns, and selling them—and himself—on the value of extension offerings. In those days when extension maintained a close if poorly defined partnership with the Farm Bureau, Hilton could build a network of valuable contacts with two statewide organizations, even if not every reception was entirely friendly. Members of the rival Farm Union organization, in Hilton's words, "were outspoken not only against the Farm Bureau, but the Extension programs, and even threatened violence."[15] Perhaps this experience had value as well, however. After the Farm Union's hostility, any future sharp rivalry was unlikely to intimidate him.

The early 1920s also had lasting influence on Hilton's life of a more personal nature. He had dated Lois Baker of Nevada, Iowa, ever since his first year at Iowa State.[16] Noticing the tall brunette in, of all places, chemistry class, Hilton asked a friend

THE SALESMAN

to introduce them. Ms. Baker found Hilton's courtly ways and southern colloquialisms somewhat bemusing, but also charming.[17] The match, lucky enough at Iowa State with its small pool of eligible coeds, proved lasting as well. Of his partner through many upheavals, Hilton declared "The greatest thing that happened to me in those years [as county agent] was when Lois and I were married on Dec. 31, 1923."[18]

The three decades that followed were good to the Hiltons. Though certainly eventful, Hilton's account of them is light on anecdotes compared with the long struggle for his first degree; whatever the period's colorful episodes, they no longer threatened to derail his entire future.

In 1926 he left the Iowa State Extension for a position as dairy extension specialist at Purdue University, where he and Lois remained for most of the next 20 years. Hilton slowly moved upward through Purdue's dairy department, taking courses toward a further degree as time permitted. In the mid-1930s he relocated to the University of Wisconsin for two years, as his advancement at Purdue had by that point precluded coursework there. Though Hilton left Madison with a M.S. degree in animal husbandry, still short of a PhD, he confided that "For reasons I will never quite understand, I received an H (highest grade) in all [classes at Wisconsin], which was far better than I ever did as a student at Purdue or Iowa State."[19]

Upon his return to Indiana in 1937, Purdue awarded Hilton a full professorship as well as the second-highest office in its dairy husbandry program. In the meantime, his private life was flourishing as well. Mrs. Hilton gave birth to the couple's first child, Elinor, in 1926, with Helen and James Gardner following. The family bought their first house in 1938. Comfortably settled in and confident of his future at Purdue, Hilton turned down multiple job offers from other land-grant institutions as the 1940s began. Even when North Carolina State invited Hilton to take charge of its department of animal industry, he said no: "It was tempting, but after several family conferences and commitments from Purdue to expand the fields of research in which I was interested, we decided to stay in Indiana."[20]

Rejection did not dissuade Hilton's ardent suitors. His reputation continued rising, steadily, in academic and scientific circles alike.[21] In 1945, Hilton accepted a doctorate of science from Purdue—and a renewed job offer from North Carolina State College. Purdue had been slow in delivering on the promises made in countering the earlier offer, while NCSC had sweetened its invitation with pledges of higher office soon to follow. America's land-grant colleges seemed agreed that James Hilton was a man of impressive talent and even greater promise.

Immediately upon starting at North Carolina State, the college asked Hilton to help in their bid for appropriations from the state legislature. The experience proved both valuable and further demonstration of advantages to his return home. To Hilton's pleasant surprise, "even though I had been away from North Carolina for almost a quarter of a century, I found that I knew many people in the state."[22] More than one old classmate had joined him in the corridors of power by this point, and welcomed him as a native returned to the fold. Best of all, attitudes in North Carolina's government were turning

THE SALESMAN

wonderfully generous with education funds at the exact moment Hilton arrived to seek them out.

As Hilton observed later, "The state of North Carolina accumulated great financial reserves during World War II." In the years which followed, its government elected to invest much of this bounty in schools. At the same time that Iowa's Governor Beardsley was determined that prosperity should not raise expectations for education budgets, a frustrated Virgil Hancher might have had the Tar Heel State foremost in mind when complaining that "While other states moved forward, Iowa held back."[23] In 1949, the same year in which Beardsley took office in Iowa, James Hilton hailed North Carolina's recent election of W. Kerr Scott, "a close personal friend" as governor. Hilton's reaction was likely pleased but not entirely surprised when, subsequently, 1949 "became the greatest year of all for state appropriations to North Carolina State College."[24]

The embarrassment of riches that Hilton enjoyed begins, by this point, to merit a pause for examination. Certainly he had good luck, including one or more propitious good-old-boy connections. Yet even combined, these seem inadequate to explain how a perpetually broke, intermittent and usually mediocre student went on to not only success, but broad success within higher education.

By the 1940s, Hilton was doubtlessly honing various talents demonstrated later as Iowa State's president. Over the years he developed into a talented leader, listener and lobbyist. I suspect, however, that a deeper personal quality played a part in Hilton's rise from the very beginning. As far back as Mr.

Riddle's intervention in the life of a teenage boy on his third job of the summer, people seem to have perceived a character in Hilton which old paper records fail to capture, except by implication. This character might constitute another legacy from materially restricted parents, particularly as James Hilton was not the only one of Henry and Alice's children to attain recognition. Hilton was named North Carolina State's dean of agriculture in 1948; not long after, at least one newspaper suggested a Hilton dynasty. Reporting Henry Hilton, Jr's resignation as director of North Carolina's personnel department to accept a job in the private sector, *The Robesonian* noted also the achievements of his older brother James. Undistinguished country folk four decades earlier, the clan were now the Catawba County Hiltons, known to be "smart folks," to boot.[25]

It's worth remembering also that James Hilton was by any fair accounting an "overnight success years in the making." By the early 1950s, North Carolina State and other schools were eyeing him as a candidate for the very top job—but Hilton was entering middle age, in the meantime, with a quarter-century of administrative experience to his credit. Iowa's Board of Education elevated Virgil Hancher to the presidency, in contrast, directly from private life at age 44.

The fact that an old friend also played a part in the board's eventual offer to Hilton, therefore, deserves to be judged in context. As Hilton remembered, one day in 1952,

> ...there appeared in my mail a penciled note on a two-cent postal card from V. B. Hamilton, a native of Tennessee with whom I had been friends when we both were students at Iowa State. He was now a member of the State Board of Regents

[*sic*] in Iowa, and he inquired if I would be interested in becoming president of Iowa State College. If so, he would like to meet with me in Gatlinburg, Tennessee, in about 10 days. I didn't take the inquiry very seriously, but the quarter was about over at North Carolina State and it was an ideal time to take a trip to the mountains, so we met as he suggested about the middle of June in 1952.[26]

Vincent B. Hamilton personally chaired the committee to determine who would succeed the outgoing Charles Friley. Yet, in Hilton's telling, Hamilton did more work selling a prospective employer to Hilton than the other way around. This account seems plausible, too, given that Hilton had already turned down Iowa State in 1949. The earlier offer had been for dean of agriculture, the same job to which North Carolina State had already promoted Hilton the year before. This time, Iowa State was proposing the presidency, and combined with Hilton's affection for the school it might have seemed that he would need little selling. Except once again, North Carolina State was increasing its attractions at the same time.

Chancellor J.W. Harrelson was due to retire from NCSC in one year, the same time as President Friley. The president of North Carolina's overall university system, Dr. Gordon Gray, later confirmed the open secret that James Hilton was in line for top posts at two major land-grant colleges at the same time. Gray noted that Hilton "was very high on the list of those who were being considered for the Chancellory of State College."[27] Other reports and Hilton's own memoir suggest that "very high" was in this case a delicate way of saying "first choice," and Gray may well have preferred to avoid specifics. By the time he spoke, after all, acknowledging that Hilton was North Carolina State's first choice meant acknowledging that they had dropped the ball.

In Hilton's telling, he simply let fate decide. It had served him well often enough, and he found little other reason to favor one job over the other. Chancellor of North Carolina State would be a tremendous honor, appropriations were bountiful, and the state was his family's home. Returning to Ames would mean uprooting his life one more time... but Iowa State had his loyalty and gratitude, still, and as its president he would report to no one else but the board. "I decided," he explained after, that "if either Iowa State or North Carolina State made a formal offer I would accept the one which came first." Whether Iowa's board proved more efficient than North Carolina's university system, as one Iowa journalist would boast[28], or the North Carolinians simply happened to respond more slowly, Iowa State's offer came first. The issue was decided. Early in 1953, Iowa State's *Alumnus* magazine beamed: "Jim is Coming Back."[29]

CHAPTER THREE
Hilton's Dream

The structure of Iowa's public higher education system may, or may not, have helped it move more efficiently than competitors in pursuing James Hilton. That system's structure and efficiency were nonetheless topics of great interest, which regularly intersected with the new president's ambitions.

Arguments over how to organize Iowa's colleges were almost as old as Iowa State, and essentially inseparable from its history. Just as many states did, Iowa created colleges in piecemeal fashion during the 19th century. It opened a university in the state capital in 1847 (leaving it behind upon transferring the capital from Iowa City to Des Moines). Eleven years later the state approved an Agricultural College and Model Farm in Ames. Iowa's acceptance of the federal Morrill Act in 1864, however, marked the real beginning of a century-long debate.

The Morrill Act authorized each state to create a land-grant college. Selecting or creating the land-grant college, or colleges, provided ready-made controversies for signatory states and Iowa was no exception. The young State University's friends lobbied hard for giving it charge of the new program. An opposing coalition scorned the idea of a school of liberal arts and professional programs, on an urban campus, teaching practical agriculture.[1] Opinion within this coalition was less united over where to establish the land-grant college instead.[2] But Iowa's demographics soundly eliminated the university viewpoint from contention, and the small college in Ames eventually emerged as one of the first land-grant institutions.

That initial victory was far from the end of tensions with the university. While the state's agricultural orientation favored the college in Ames, State University of Iowa's enrollment was consistently higher and therefore productive of more alumni, whose lawyers and other professionals tended to occupy offices of influence. Emergence as the state's football power did nothing to hurt SUI's popularity.[3] A third institution complicated the picture, meanwhile, when Iowa State Normal School opened in Cedar Falls in 1876. As its own official history allows, the school's location independent of both older institutions was a pure product of local opportunism and political dexterity.[4] It was there, all the same, and though firmly relegated to third place in budget and enrollment by 1900 it had an impact disproportionate to its size. By firmly establishing the idea of three state schools—three touchy communities of students, employees, neighbors and alumni—the teachers college effectively ruled out the possibility of any one school ever gaining complete dominance.

Iowa's institutions of higher education were thus relatively free to develop as they liked. Each had an administration and even a board of its own. All three still had the same paymaster in the form of the legislature, however, and this provided an ongoing source of contention. Each school was fiercely protective of its own rights and privileges, and Iowans in general were content to respect these. But Iowa's lawmakers were perennially convinced that any program found at two or more of the schools could be provided more cheaply at just one.

In theory all three schools had distinct roles, which should have naturally guided their development away from duplication of effort. In practice, by the beginning of the 20th century the scope for cost-cutting efficiencies appeared considerable. The college in Ames, renamed Iowa State College of Agriculture and Mechanic Arts, emphasized technical subjects—but State University of Iowa awarded engineering degrees also. Both Iowa State Teachers College and SUI trained teachers. Home economics coursework, under various names, turned up at all three schools along with assorted science and humanities programs. Seeing no hope of three separate school boards curtailing their charges' ambitions, Iowa replaced them in 1909 with one State Board of Education.

The board went straight to work on the problem of "duplication" that had prompted its creation, and within three years proposed a comprehensive solution. The state should base engineering coursework in Ames, and close State University of Iowa's program. In turn, Iowa State should cede domestic sciences to SUI. The Teachers College and SUI would split teacher training, with upperclass work concentrated in Iowa City.

The new board succeeded in uniting Iowa's higher education interests immediately—in opposition. None had welcomed the mere formal usurpation of their old autonomy, even before the board's 1912 proposal. All were incensed at the suggestion they should now surrender actual, functioning departments, each a result of great investment and effort. If any potential existed to recruit Iowa State College and State University of Iowa to the plan's general goals, by bargaining over details, the objections of Iowa State Teachers College ruled out any compromise. If all Teachers College students had to complete their studies at State University of Iowa, and most could also commence them there, then ISTC would soon be reduced to a junior college and possibly to nonexistence.[5] In all likelihood Iowa State and the university probably needed little urging from ISTC, anyway. The tribes of all three schools reacted with such fury that the board was soon isolated. Both candidates for governor denounced the plan. The legislature passed a joint resolution not only declaring the plan "unwise," but explicitly endorsing duplication, at least "to such extent as will advance the educational interests of the state."[6]

The Board of Education inevitably backed down. Just as inevitably, Iowa's colleges took the legislature at its word and began opening even more duplicative departments. The board, still owing its whole existence to the goal of battling duplication, found itself in one of the most basic political conundrums: everyone opposes wasteful spending as a category, but every specific expenditure has beneficiaries who see nothing wasteful about it. The board responded as politicians often respond when confronting unpopular tasks, by commissioning a study.

The result of 40 more years of studies and committees was an uneasy peace, as President James Hilton took office with grand goals for Iowa State College. Multiple commissions had suggested that duplication was more of a neutral phenomenon to be managed, than a peril to be eliminated, and the board quickly distanced itself from the rare study that concluded otherwise.[7] The studies' two chief, cumulative legacies had a mixed impact. Their formal legacy was a concept of "major" and "service" departments. Where duplication proved difficult to avoid completely, for one reason or another, this model advised that degrees in the duplicating subject be restricted to one school, and that other schools' offerings remain supportive "service courses," only. Less formally, even as multiple studies praised the modest results of this policy, those reports were at the same time constant reminders that Iowa governments remained suspicious of duplicating programs, whatever they were called.

This common antagonist had helped, gradually, to resign the state schools to board leadership. Where the board of 1912 had never provided Iowa's college administrators anything but interference, by 1953 all three presidents owed their jobs to the Board of Education. Combined with a gentler hand on duplication, the schools were generally content to regard the board, and each other, as necessary allies in dealing with outside threats.

Chief among these were invariably Iowa's lawmakers. Neither the new governor nor the biennial assemblies were proving significantly more generous than had the late Governor Beardsley. In 1951, President Hancher was reduced to insisting "This figure did not come out of a hat" in arguing for increased funding.[8] Amid increasing competition for faculty, State University of Iowa's salaries were last among the "Big Ten" Western Conference schools, yet legislators remained skeptical. Despite regular protest by the board, Iowa's Budget and Financial Control Committee and the pre-audit system remained in place. All told, the situation greeting Hancher's new opposite number at Iowa State was vastly different from what he'd left behind. Within six months of taking office, President Hilton shared in a general order from the powerful Control Committee to find money-saving efficiencies.[9] Presented with barely one-third of his first capital improvements request, two years later, Hilton declared "this is a sad, sad story."[10]

Yet Hilton certainly knew in advance what he was getting himself into. Though his public comments upon becoming president were consistently positive, he had not returned to Iowa State without reading a newspaper or asking a single question. Quite possibly the conditions in Iowa contributed to the Board of Education's difficult time in simply getting Hilton to the point where he was willing to take their offer or leave it, depending on chance. In its final salary offer of $18,500 per year, the board had in fact promised Hilton $2,500 more than it had ever paid an employee. (It raised salaries for Presidents Hancher and Friley to the same level, upon Hilton's acceptance.[11]) This demonstration of the board's backing, however, did not blind Hilton to the parsimony prevailing more generally.

One of his first decisions as president was refusing traditional installation pageantry.[12] The board actually argued for

HILTON'S DREAM

being more liberal here, too, but Hilton made the decision stick. At the ordinary staff convocation that marked his arrival instead, he made clear that he planned on being a fighter. But he was going to choose his battles. Though he had pointed to the college's approaching centenary as a better use for installation ceremony funds, I suspect that Hilton also had another symbolic purpose in mind. He very much planned grand programs for Iowa State under his tenure. He would need to show respect to the budgetary preference for thrift, however, first.

Like President Hancher, Hilton arrived in office with tall ambitions. Also like Hancher he promptly met with distractions large and small. Fans were so dissatisfied with Cyclone athletics, and football in particular, that when Hilton made a formal statement a few months into the fall of 1953 the student newspaper employed the language of scandal: "President James H. Hilton broke a three-day silence on the part of the college Saturday," according to the *Iowa State Daily*.[13] One of the season's rare victories only produced an even bigger headache. Following a Homecoming game win, students expected a school holiday. Hilton questioned this "tradition," apparently an innovation since his own undergraduate days, and suggested that the suspension of Friday afternoon and Saturday morning classes was already sufficient holiday. Hundreds and eventually thousands of students then protested before Hilton worked out a compromise, to suspend Monday classes after future Homecoming games, win or lose. To the president's further chagrin, the episode made *LIFE* magazine.[14] (The mysterious

James H. Hilton, c. 1950.
University Photographs, Box 63, Iowa State University Library Special Collections.

tradition of canceling classes for Homecoming has since fallen into abeyance.)

Happily for the new president and everyone else, he was spared a mobilization for war, unlike President Hancher a dozen years earlier. Hilton's first years nonetheless played out during the worst of the McCarthy period, as well as the broader Cold War era. When one Iowa State junior decided that his industrial management textbook advocated leftist theories, the *Wall Street Journal* published both his letter of warning and an editorial amplifying the issue. Following a deluge of letters and telegrams, Hilton's response only enlarged the fiasco. The *Journal*'s publication of his own letter—as Hilton later realized he should have expected—only prompted a second round of uproar.[15]

While Iowa's newest college president was stumbling, the senior president was enjoying a recovery from his own trials. In 1951, a colleague in the Association of American Universities congratulated President Hancher on a story that State University of New York was hiring him away[16]; the rumor proved false but Hancher's reputation was rising all the same. When a national magazine featured Hancher the following year, it was with admiration rather than smirks. Calling Hancher "one of the top university presidents in the U.S.," *Time* lauded him as a man of intellect, influence and accomplishment.[17]

The 1952 profile by *Time* paid tribute to the results of 12 years' perseverance through the frustrations that still awaited James Hilton. The story praised a beginning at "remodeling his curriculum, slashing away at the hodgepodge of vocational courses in favor of a broad and solid liberal arts program," reforms Hancher had desired since his own early presidency.

HANCHER VS. HILTON

It acknowledged the College of Nursing, and the school for handicapped children opened under Hancher's leadership. Along with these earlier projects, *Time* reported more recent progress on a university library, and a communications center. Notably, both were designed for gradual expansion by stages[18]—reflecting Hancher's adjusted expectations for resources. Even while enjoying the applause of national media, President Hancher remained sensitive to tougher audiences closer to home.

In North Carolina, Hilton had been able to move quickly and count on broad support. After just five years as dean of agriculture, he enjoyed credit for "great strides" toward the top ranks of land-grant institutions.[19] At Iowa State, he was taking charge of an institution which he already regarded as among the best of its kind, and any improvements that he could propose would obviously take longer to fund. Nonetheless, in nearly every other way, I believe that Hilton approached his presidency exactly the same at Iowa State as he would have done at North Carolina State College.

As dean of agriculture, Hilton's leadership had in fact been cautious and considered in approach. He made a point of listening—and just as important of demonstrating that he was listening—carefully to broad audiences before announcing any major initiative. Once convinced that a goal aligned with interests of the community he took to the circuit again, selling it to every audience who would have him.[20] Even advanced to formal authority and power, Hilton's method clearly harkened back to his days as a county agent in rural Iowa, and people seemed appreciative of the approach. When the time came to seek public funds, friendships absolutely helped get results quickly. But Hilton also helped himself by cultivating friendships at every opportunity.

President Hilton saw no need to adjust his style for a new institution and comparatively frail local ties. "Following certain basic principles of administration which had paid large dividends in North Carolina," he determined, "I felt sure I could make progress in Iowa."[21] Only in the pace of progress did he expect to make concessions. As dean of agriculture at North Carolina State, he had achieved a transformation in five years. At Iowa State, though he held a much higher office, he titled his eventual agenda "Iowa State College Ten Years From Now."

In every other way the blueprint that Hilton unveiled after 10 months' consultation with legislators, citizens and the university community was bold, even brazen. The president called for a substantially expanded operating budget, especially for salaries that had fallen behind at Iowa State, just as at SUI. His plan also encompassed more than 25 new buildings. Most incredible of all, to observers, was the handful of buildings designated for a completely new cultural center. Iowa State College had nothing remotely like this—as Hilton had noted while touring the campus his first weekend back in Ames. Human users shared the gymnasium with families of sparrows. The student union was a warren, thanks to repeated additions, none of which could accommodate a truly large event at once. In the cavernous Armory events had plenty of room, but "You couldn't hear very well unless you were in the front four or five [rows]."[22]

Hilton argued that both Iowa State and the state of Iowa owed themselves better. With a large auditorium, a more intimate theater and a great coliseum, ISC could host prominent lecturers and performers along with the larger audiences to make their visits worthwhile. Adjacent space for meetings and continuing education would underscore the cultural center's value to the broader community.

When President Hilton first announced all of this it was met with disbelief. Virgil Hancher had spent most of 15 years lobbying for new construction including an auditorium at the state's larger "flagship" school, and gone gray in winning even a part of those askings.[23] The name "Hilton's Dream" stuck to the proposal before long, but even at Iowa State many felt that "fantasy" or "delusion" might be more appropriate terms. The day after Hilton first presented his vision to faculty, an anonymous donor sent the president a two-dollar bill.[24] It's very possible that this was some joker's way of way of saying, politely, *good luck with that*.

Hilton had proposed that private gifts and other outside funds might pay for the "Iowa State College Center," and with his relentless optimism and a touch of good humor, he chose to embrace the anonymous foundation gift. He also suggested, with more precedent, that student residence construction would pay for itself. But even if these hopes were achieved, and state funds were reserved for the classrooms that Hilton insisted must be first priority, the necessary appropriations seemed impossible. Over and over Hilton heard the question: where would that money come from? "That was not the question in my mind," was his straightforward answer. "These were

HILTON'S DREAM

the needs, and the financial resources would have to be found somewhere."[25]

Both the scale of "Hilton's Dream" and his certainty in the face of all doubts were, in their way, breathtaking. Even if they were delusional, they were captivating visions. They were also troubling visions, however, in a context of pre-auditing, constant sensitivity to duplication, and a generally delicate relationship among Iowa's colleges and its lawmakers. Regardless of who paid for it, an expansive, expensive cultural center was not the project of a specialized technical school, content in ceding preeminence to the senior institution.

CHAPTER FOUR

Collegiality

James Hilton's aggressive plans for Iowa State College were startling, by themselves. Their author was a quintessential booster and took every opportunity to draw even more attention to them. Remarkably, relations with State University of Iowa were undisturbed by the news.

President Hancher's wariness of state college ambitions had certainly not gone away. Yet somehow nearly five years passed in peace. Negligible progress on Hilton's building agenda may have reassured Hancher that harsh reality was making it unnecessary to voice his own concerns. As might the fact that on one key issue, Hilton himself seemed to share his colleague's skepticism. In a growing number of other states, land-grant colleges were beginning to agitate for university status, and the Iowa State community soon felt the same stirrings. But for the time being James Hilton's reaction was to argue against the idea. He simply didn't see the need. Iowa State already had many attributes of a university, and Hilton was quite ready to acquire more, but he felt that changing the school's name would not materially aid in the process and might distract from it.

The two men's attitudes weren't entirely compatible, but Hancher's aim was ultimately to avoid a competition. If Iowa State's president opposed formally establishing a second state university, in the face of mounting pressure, Hancher had little reason to pick a fight.

Both presidents, inevitably, had other things to occupy them.

In the mid-1950s, Hilton may have regarded Iowa State's name as a distraction he could ignore in part because he faced other distractions he could not. Discontent over Cyclone athletics continued to simmer. Reconciling a growing desire to park cars on campus and a limited number of spaces was proving a match for even Hilton's unsinkable optimism.[1] In 1957 a more acute crisis erupted over yet another dubious tradition, this time in the form of the "panty raid."

Even in the feminism-light 1950s, patience was already wearing thin with the fad for male students invading women's dormitories. Following weeks of chatter, one planned "raid" became an open secret throughout campus, and the Hilton administration issued a clear warning: anyone leading the rumored stunt would be punished. Freshman John Marshal obligingly called the authorities' bluff. Unfortunately for him they were not bluffing, and suspended Marshal for the remainder of the school year, citing "quite a little damage to two of the dormitories"[2] alongside his disregard for an official warning.

COLLEGIALITY

Marshal's family then protested loudly. As Verne Marshal was a former editor of the *Gazette*, he received a flurry of press coverage as well as a letter of support from a state senator. In the end, though, the recently renamed Board of Regents backed President Hilton and upheld the suspension. It was some small progress from Hilton's earlier concessions to student immaturity, even if it was another embarrassing episode.

Newspaper sensationalism and grandstanding politicians took another shot at President Hancher as well, around the same time. In 1956 the Regents approved spending $16,000 on a golf lift for the university's Finkbine course. The money was earmarked from athletic funds—which rules prohibited spending on other university priorities—and the coin-operated device would dependably repay its cost over time. But critics did not let fine distinctions restrain them. Board member Roy Stevens cast a dissenting vote, complaining that the purchase could not possibly square with the university's claimed needs in other departments.[3] State Senator George O'Malley echoed the complaint; as did a *Des Moines Register* editorial, which protested a new press box at Iowa Stadium as well. The Hancher administration wearily explained the realities of the purchases, as well as the facts that the press itself had voted SUI's press box "worst in the nation for several years" and that the site of the golf lift had been popularly christened "Cardiac Hill."[4]

Although Hancher had not found time to set foot on a golf course in years, he may have winced at this last detail afterward. Even as media continued toying with ridicule of the golf lift, nearly a year after its announcement, jokes about heart problems became suddenly less frivolous. On November

17, 1956, State University of Iowa's president suffered a heart attack. The incident was fortunately mild, in relative terms; Hancher began feeling ill at a Hawkeye football contest with Ohio State, but did not suspect anything life-threatening and remained through the game's finish (a 6-0 upset win by SUI). A visit to his doctor afterward produced the more worrying diagnosis that the president had suffered a "mild coronary occlusion."[5]

One juvenile newspaper editor made light of the entire episode, with the headline "Iowa U President Gets Too Excited,"[6] but Hancher's attitude was far less cavalier. With limitless potential responsibilities he had grown accustomed to working in one form or another morning, noon and night[7], but all that changed immediately. Though back to the office by the following winter, he drastically cut back his schedule for months.[8]

Some larger issues took an unwelcome turn, as well, during these years. One newspaper's report of President Hancher's improving health appeared only two columns from a headline unlikely to provide any further comfort, predicting a "Tidal Wave of College Students in Country by 1970."[9] This forecast was even more frightening given the new governor's stance on higher education funding. In his determination to shave a half-percent off Iowa's sales tax rate, Governor Herschel Loveless appeared to surpass Beardsley's antipathy toward the Regents. In 1957 the Iowa legislature approved approximately $11 million for capital spending by the Regents institutions; Loveless then vetoed it along with other capital improvements appropriations. For the next two years Iowa's colleges went without a single cent for improving their campus infrastructure. Faced with considerable criticism, Loveless blustered about how the schools ought to economize. Naturally he included obligatory complaints about duplication, asking "why both the university and Iowa State educate engineers, and whether it could be done more efficiently at one of the schools."[10]

At the same time, the news was not entirely bad. Hawkeye football was on an upswing, making a victorious trip to the Rose Bowl after the 1956 season. The Cold War continued to loom in the background, but the worst of the domestic witch-hunts and suspicion appeared to be ending, as Hilton acknowledged with relief in his 1955 convocation remarks.[11] Relationships with lawmakers showed signs of improvement too, even allowing for the governor's hostility. By 1956 Hilton believed that "in all sincerity, there has been a big change in the thinking and attitude of members of the legislature toward the needs of these institutions of higher learning since the 1955 session. More people, and certainly more members of both the Senate and House, are genuinely seeking ways of meeting these responsibilities than perhaps [at] any time in our history."[12] Recent assemblies had appropriated somewhat larger operating budgets, and although the governor had revoked their pledged capital funding, this was still evidence of progress.[13]

The slow, quiet repeal of the pre-audit system represented another encouraging gesture. Since 1951, the Board of Regents and the institutions in their charge had openly resisted the requirement to suspend any proposed purchase until authorized by the state's pre-auditor. Board secretary Dave Dancer said the program was neither necessary, nor good government, and was costing money rather than saving it by holding up payments so long that schools were losing potential cash discounts and incurring late-payment fees. President Hancher called the system pure red tape, and approved State University of Iowa's treasurer flagrantly bypassing it entirely. With the board's blessing, SUI and other schools simply began issuing payments after a perfunctory delay. Such was the intensity of administrators' disgust with pre-auditing that they purchased literal rubber stamps, to mark payments made in advance of formal approval, saying "I certify that the pre-auditor has had the opportunity to pre-audit this voucher in accordance with the law."[14]

This hardly seemed calculated to win over the General Assembly, yet lawmakers were distancing themselves from pre-auditing rather than digging in. It may be that some legislators couldn't help seeing the humor. If others were less pleased with blatant mockery of the law, a growing number of them concluded that it was just not worth defending. The same Senator O'Malley, who insisted that SUI's golf lift constituted indefensible wasteful spending, washed his hands of pre-auditing; even he found no evidence the law had "saved the state of Iowa a dime."[15] A repeal stalled in 1955, even after 40-3 approval in the Senate. But two years later, repeal of pre-auditing breezed through the assembly without a single opposing Senate vote.[16]

Taken altogether, the job of running Iowa's public universities (official and otherwise) seemed to be growing more cordial by the late 1950s. Iowa State administrators very naturally expressed shock at President Hancher's heart attack, and sent wishes for a speedy recovery.[17] Correspondence on business matters was generally warm as well, even on the touchy subject of duplication. The Regents schools were holding ongoing interinstitutional committee meetings; at one point Iowa State Teachers College's dean of instruction sent colleagues a draft course catalog for examination, noting specially that "we have dropped all of the courses in Agriculture in accordance with the approval of the State Board of Regents, and we will leave that field strictly to Iowa State College."[18]

In late 1957 the Association of American Universities finally overcame years of inertia to extend offers of membership to four more institutions, and with broad support Iowa State became the first "college" on its rolls.[19] President Hancher sent a congratulatory letter.[20] His remarks at Iowa State's centennial observances the following spring, commending the college's unique importance in Iowa public education, seemed to confirm his sincerity.

Considered in context, I'm inclined to see genuine goodwill in Hancher's comments and letter of congratulations, as well as in Hilton's response that "we shall forever be grateful."[21] Just weeks before the centennial event, the student senate had endorsed renaming the school Iowa State University. But Hilton—who had some reason to question student judgment by that point—remained unpersuaded. For the time being, SUI's monopoly on the title of "university" was safe. Hancher's expression of friendship seems, therefore, likely to have been just as sincere as his tribute to Iowa State's distinct non-university role in higher education.

The two presidents' outward accord was, all the same, still only circumstantial. The underlying visions were simply incompatible, and if neither man pressed this point, Hilton had not sought to conceal it either. Amid his comments, Hancher had declared it "the function of the three publicly-supported institutions to complement, rather than supplant, the other institutions in the state."[22] Though he thanked Hancher afterward, Hilton emphasized a rather different outlook. "From time to time institutions, like individuals must pass through critical periods as they grow and mature and move from one situation to another," he said. Iowa State College, Hilton reminded his guests, "was born of change, and it will continue to alter its thinking and its methods to meet those problems which are still ahead of us."[23] Intentional or not this was a warning, even more plain than "Hilton's Dream," that goodwill dependent on the status quo could not last forever.

CHAPTER FIVE
Rupture

Throughout 1958 President Hilton continued to pursue more concrete changes to Iowa State College, while ruminating on a revised name. His first priorities were, still, mostly compatible with the idea of Iowa State as a specialist institution. He looked to get the Center for Agricultural and Economic Adjustment, opened the previous year, off to a strong start. This and the National Animal Disease Lab, which ISC had recently helped win for the city of Ames, were firm demonstrations of the school's commitment to serving the public through agricultural research. Expansion of atomic studies at Ames Lab likewise fit neatly within the purview of a non-university technical institute.

All the same, if Hilton was not yet persuaded that Iowa State needed to call itself a university, he was convinced that it *was* a university and had every claim to develop and grow as a university. President Hancher had a fundamentally different view. In the spring of 1958, each had hinted at this in his public remarks. In the first third of 1959 both men made these differences explicit, at least to a select audience. If any single event in the conflict of Hancher vs. Hilton constituted an open "declaration of war," it was a February 20, 1959 memo titled "Suggestions on Future Directions for Development of Our Three Institutions."

Early that year, the Board of Regents had tasked all three state schools with working out coordinated plans for growth. It was realistically the kind of exercise that might have produced nothing but vague statements of intent, free of any binding commitment, politely approved and then filed while its authors proceeded unconstrained in their individual courses. A first draft by Iowa State Teachers College president William Maucker pointed in precisely this direction. Maucker's main suggestion was essentially to list several liberal arts fields, which he regarded as obvious areas for expanding ISTC's and Iowa State College's degree offerings. President Hancher's lengthy response was an unequivocal, withering disapproval. Whether happily or not, Hancher had accepted Iowa State joining the AAU. But in every other regard he maintained all the objections he had expressed privately eight years earlier:

> ...I see nothing imaginative or creative, nothing qualitative or excellent in this approach. We shall merely be following the prevailing practice throughout the United States under which any publicly supported institution, created for a special purpose, whether it be a technical institute, a normal school, a teachers college, or a land-grant college, abandons the specialized purpose for which it was created or puts that purpose far to one side in order to become a general university. The

RUPTURE

resulting multiplication of universities engenders duplication and competition which must inevitably lower the quality of higher education and which the general public is finding and in the future will continue to find increasingly and intolerably expensive. ... As a result there is a growing public feeling that higher educational institutions are wasteful, competitive and over-supported and that they and their governing boards must be brought to heel...[1]

In a sense, Hancher was adopting Hilton's own attitude to that point, i.e. that whether or not Iowa State was classified as "a university" was unimportant. Whether college or university, it was to Hancher's thinking fundamentally distinct from State University of Iowa. It had been specifically created to be distinct; Hancher pointed out that founders of both ISC and ISTC had insisted on organizing them separately from SUI, on the grounds that a liberal arts university could not offer the focus necessary for their specialized fields. "Now we are told that it cannot exist apart from such a setting," and yet, he pondered, "Will these latter views prove to be as wrong in fifty or seventy-five years as the older views are now thought to be?"[2]

To the extent that Iowa State or the Teachers College already offered liberal arts curricula, Hancher denied that this necessitated offering liberal arts degrees. Instead he proposed that the whole concept of relying on distinct liberal arts classes, to provide a liberal education to scientists and technicians, needed rethinking. To his mind this was a peculiarity of American education, clumsy and expensive; administrators should examine the model of European education such as his own

77

studies at Oxford, a theme which he would develop further in the years ahead. In the meantime the imperfect compromise of service courses in liberal arts and humanities should not be discarded on a whim. As he warned in a follow-up memo, "it would be unwise to assume that legislative concern with duplication, which provides the background for all the Regents' activities in this connection and for their successive studies and reports, has been wholly dissipated by the lapse of time."[3]

For Hancher, the core issue was that every expansion of liberal arts and humanities at other public schools would be inherently harmful to State University of Iowa. For SUI the liberal arts were not a sideline but a speciality, every bit as much as law or medicine, or engineering at Iowa State, or teaching at ISTC. Given the consistent scarcity of state appropriations, the creation of two more liberal arts colleges would inevitably water down that of SUI. Iowa's population was growing slowly and funding for higher education was likely to do the same. "The University can testify to the difficulty of maintaining one general college of liberal arts," Hancher declared. "What reason is there to expect that three will be… even as well supported?"[4] The result would certainly be underfunded, poor-quality liberal arts colleges—which would clearly hurt State University of Iowa most of all.

The insouciance of his colleagues toward this threat offended Hancher, deeply. "On more than one occasion," he pointed out, "bills have been introduced in the General Assembly by persons hostile to the University for the purpose of abolishing engineering at the University." But no alumnus or friend "so far as it is known has tried to kill home economics at ISU or college level teacher training at ISTC!" Why were the liberal arts fair game, then? To drive home his point he offered a counter-example: "...if a similar suggestion were made by ISTC and SUI concerning the Division of Agriculture at ISC (and in the foremost agricultural state in the Union a good case could be made for exposing all of our students to agriculture) the reaction of ISC to the proposal would be essentially negative, and rightly so."[5]

The appropriate solution, Hancher proposed, was much deeper coordination. President Maucker's original memo had criticized negotiations between Regents institutions, to leave this or that major alone, as an "essentially negative approach." Hancher agreed, but rather than casting off restraint, his prescription was to cede all responsibility for curriculum development to a central authority. Instead of the Board of Regents acting as arbitrators when schools disagreed, a single office should determine policy for all of the schools in the first place. Curriculum, academic calendar, salaries, hiring and promotion policies, extension, even student visits...

Though Hancher professed neutrality on whether this proposal functioned as "one institution with three campuses or as three institutions forming an integrated system," the outcome would be essentially the same. In concluding his memo he outlined suggested missions for all three schools, and the very phrasing illuminates his concept of SUI's sister institutions: "1. Ames - This institution or campus would be a technological and agricultural institution of the highest rank, comparable to the CA Institute of Technology and the Massachusetts Institute of Technology..."[6]

HANCHER VS. HILTON

Virgil Hancher was not given to using exclamation points. His use of one in a formal memo, perhaps the product of long-simmering frustration at last boiling over, is almost shocking. Though his arguments were both pointed and challenging, he was obviously angry.

The response which he provoked has quite a different character. Hilton, I suspect, brooded over "Some Reactions to President Hancher's Memorandum..."[7] His own comments have a character of painstaking precision. Every bit the equal of its target in thoroughness, Hilton's reply goes Hancher one better in fact, with copious footnotes mostly keyed to Hancher's original comments. Hilton, it appears, sought less to reply to Hancher's arguments than to demolish them, as cleanly, respectfully and professionally as possible.

Hilton's core argument was that, contra President Hancher, technical specialization was not Iowa State's central identity and never had been. Comparing Iowa State College with MIT demonstrated a complete misunderstanding of the land-grant system, Hilton asserted. Iowa State's special purpose was *being a land-grant college*, a distinct category itself, defined above all by service to the public and encompassing basic sciences from the very beginning. As for the suggestion that granting degrees in the humanities represented a Rubicon, Hilton pointed out that Iowa State had offered majors in history, sociology, economics and other social sciences as long ago as the 1920s. "In short," he replied to President Hancher, "our program... is not, as the statement implies, the result of a new 'expansionist fashion' in 'educational thinking,' which is 'sweeping over the country.'"[8] Neither would it mean abandoning specialties that, if not the totality of Iowa State's purpose, were still traditional strengths. As evidence, Hilton listed the Center for Agricultural and Economic Adjustment, the Animal Disease Laboratory and other programs, along with 3,000 engineering students out of a total enrollment slightly more than 9,000.

Hilton further argued that expanded arts and humanities offerings, rather than distracting from applied sciences, actually support them. In a recent report that Hilton cited, the American Society for Engineering Education had called for at least one-fifth of engineering curricula to consist of social sciences and humanities. Hilton seconded this endorsement, and suggested that genuinely useful progress by applied sciences depended on collaboration with social sciences. The Center for Agricultural and Economic Adjustment, for example, "could not have been established at Iowa State, and could certainly not have been operated successfully, if this institution had not had strong departments in the basic academic disciplines."[9] Expanding on this, Hilton rejected the service course compromise as a failed experiment. Qualified scholars, he insisted, were simply not satisfied teaching for departments restricted to non-major supportive roles.

In the years that followed, Hilton returned often to this thesis, which turned on their heads two of Hancher's own concerns. Because faculty attached considerable value to a genuine major program in their field, they demanded higher salaries to work for a "service" department; thus, Hilton implied, prohibiting duplicate major programs could raise costs rather than lowering them. Even if more money for salaries could be relied on, as Hancher warned against doing, Hilton's experience was that money alone was still inadequate for truly great teachers. They would not be satisfied with an exclusively service-course role. As a result, insisting on such limitations invited the very mediocrity that Hancher decried.

For other of Hancher's theses, though, Hilton omitted any direct reply. Generally concerning himself with practical, concrete factors, Hilton offered no real answer to the proposal that relying on separate liberal arts classes to achieve liberal education is inherently simplistic and wasteful. He made no direct answer to Hancher's concern that competing liberal arts departments would erode one of SUI's own special emphases, either—though in this case, Hilton challenged the entire premise instead. "President Hancher," he wrote, "in the underlying tone of his whole statement, seemingly makes the assumption that SUI has some peculiar monopoly on the basic academic disciplines... which he repeatedly indicates are SUI's own exclusive province." Hilton rejected every part of this. No such monopoly existed in practice, as he illustrated with the references to decades-old ISC majors in social sciences. Nor was such a monopoly remotely reasonable in theory: "...no institution, public or private, can reasonably assert a monopoly over the basic academic disciplines."[10]

Having staked out positions as incompatible as this, the potential for conflict now greatly exceeded potential for compromise. President Hancher pointed to expanded duplication in liberal arts and humanities, and foretold erosion of quality, rising expense and public backlash. President Hilton thoroughly rejected Hancher's premises, predictions and prescriptions alike. With the exchange of the "Future Directions" memos in early 1959, a course toward public conflict was essentially fixed. Less than one year earlier, two men had stood side by side and expressed admiration and hopes of cooperation. Now, attached to irreconcilable views, the only plausible path toward resolution would involve turning to third parties.

At the same time Hilton was defending Iowa State College's functional identity, he was at last giving way on its symbolic identity. The decision had been a long time coming, in every sense. A full half-century earlier State University of Iowa's President MacLean had warned that the land-grant college's development pointed inevitably to university status. By then it had already offered studies and even graduate programs in literature, philosophy, and social science for a generation.[11] Iowa State rejected proposed department closings in 1913, even when offered a monopoly on engineering curricula in exchange. The Board of Education's revised, preventative policy had slowed the emergence of a university in Ames, but that was all. Iowa State College's "divisions" became colleges themselves in all but name; its graduate college made it official. The terminology imposed by history or political pressure had little practical effect on perceptions. Iowa State was generally recognized as a peer to officially titled universities, and a distinguished one. Even before it won a place in the Association of American Universities in 1958, the AAU had considered it a serious candidate for years.

Given all this, however, Hilton just did not see what need existed for a new name. He recognized a few, more specific concerns, but his core question was ultimately: why tinker with what worked fine? Iowa State was a university that happened to be called Iowa State College. Everyone knew that, everyone understood it, and renaming the school seemed more likely to create confusion than to dispel it. Hilton acknowledged the arguments in favor of relabeling divisions as colleges, and the college itself as a university. But he hesitated at personally endorsing the second step. Iowa State College was a national and even international "brand," and Hilton was essentially reluctant to risk the equity in that brand.[12] Further, for reasons of both continuity and respect to the school's deeper identity, Hilton would not consider a name that wasn't some form of "Iowa State," and joining this with "University" would not leave much room to stay clear of "State University of Iowa."[13]

Hilton remained willing to listen to alternate points of view. The student senate's recommendation was solidly backed by Iowa State's deans, including Dean of Instruction Robert Parks, whose abilities Hilton found increasingly impressive.[14] Through 1958, though, Hilton himself remained on the fence. While much of ISC's administration favored the change, Science Division Dean Richard Bear noted that while technically inaccurate, the term "state college" emphasized Iowa State's identity as one of the many land-grant institutions using the same term.[15] This point must have carried much weight with the president, given his veneration of the land-grant tradition.

For that same reason, I feel confident that the emerging trend among other members of that tradition finally dispelled Hilton's doubts. When Hilton took office as president, the "state university" was still a rarity among land-grant state colleges. Within just five years, the situation was completely reversed. State colleges had become universities in Colorado (1957), Michigan (1955), Mississippi (1958), Oklahoma (1957), Pennsylvania (1953), and Utah (1957). Combined with the handful of older land-grant universities, these exceptions were now becoming the majority; active proposals in even more states appeared likely to extend their lead.

More than the previous year's endorsement by student government, or those of the faculty council, general faculty and alumni association in early 1959, this persuaded Hilton. A press release launching the formal campaign for a new name noted that Iowa State's president "gave as his opinion that until recently the matter of the name had not been a serious matter," but with the land-grant system clearly favoring an alternate view of things, "The term 'state college' is rapidly becoming obsolete..."[16] In its place, "state university" was plainly going to be the new badge of land-grant institutions.

Iowa, however, already had a State University. As Bear had noted along with other reasons for caution, this would unavoidably mean certain "well known difficulties."

Iowa State College's own argument for becoming Iowa State University was primarily the same reasoning that had persuaded Hilton. The school was a university in reality; being a "state college" had still worked, so long as the term remained in widespread use by similar institutions, but that was no longer the case.

News releases and memos suggested various other arguments for good measure. As with service courses, faculty were alleged to be growing reluctant to "step down" from a university to work for a college. The term was also a growing impediment in pursuing federal and private grants. Set against this, the school emphasized repeatedly that the move "would not increase costs." Citing the school's international connections,

Iowa State also asserted that contrary to President Hilton's early concerns about brand recognition, the "state college" convention had long confused foreign students and scholars. The school also argued that the "Agriculture and Mechanic Arts" of its full name was equally misleading,[17] though this met with little dissent anyway. Nearly all of the "difficulties" had to do, instead, with the first part of the school's proposed name.

For President Virgil Hancher, the word "university" itself still did not belong in Ames in any form. His view remained that Iowa had one public university, and neither needed nor had means to support a second. If Iowa State College was already more a university than not, formalizing that status would still be a further step in the wrong direction. Besides Hancher, relatively few shared this concern, though. For most of the skeptics, the greater problem involved Iowa having two institutions formally called State University. Many insisted that this would be confusing; some, at least, suspected that it would also be unconstitutional.

The question of confusion was difficult to dismiss. Iowa State pointed out that confusion already existed, and this was quite true. Even before the public debate about its name, "In a single week, one department of Iowa State received 43 letters addressed to 'Iowa State University,'" the school reported. What was more, "Strangely enough, some of these letters came from other official departments of government in Iowa."[18] Even Iowa's legal code referred to Iowa State under varying names; under the circumstances, formally renaming ISC would actually permit cleaning up some of the confusion that already existed.

RUPTURE

A handwritten note suggests that Hilton found the whole issue of confusion increasingly frustrating. Perhaps also recalling President Hancher's rebuke for going along with what he considered "fads," Hilton asked:

> What is wrong with following the crowd if the crowd is right and their cause is just. There are genuine historical reasons in the Land-Grant system for retaining the word 'state' in their names. Just because the word state happens to be in the name of both institutions is no reason why Iowa State should be denied the right to have a name properly descriptive of its functions.[19]

Land-grant colleges in other states were, as Iowa State liked to point out, becoming State Universities without chaos ensuing. But each of those new State Universities was the only school in its state using the phrase. In Iowa, that would not be the case. Various observers pointed out that Iowa State had often been called "Ames College" at one time, and asked why it could not restore a similar pattern as a university. Hilton remained adamant that Iowa State University was the only reasonable name, however. Its name must contain the word "state" out of respect for its long association with land-grant institutions[20], and of course introducing the word "university" was the whole point. Reminded that Purdue and Cornell were both land-grant schools, Iowa State responded that both names predated the eventual pattern of naming such institutions for their states, and that even they were named for a founder or benefactor rather than a city. "The name Ames University would misidentify Iowa State as a municipal university, such as the University of Kansas City. Iowa State does not belong to the residents of Ames. It is a state institution, belonging to all the people of Iowa..."[21]

Hilton's note decreed that all of this was largely academic, and that in practice "We will continue to be known as 'Iowa State' and 'the university' as the 'State university' or the 'university of Iowa,'"[22] as newspapers often called the Iowa City school. This suggestion nonetheless seems to demonstrate concerns about confusion, as much as it refutes them. On the issue of two State Universities, ultimately Hilton could do little more than push ahead and insist things would work out somehow.

Fortunately Iowa State was on safer ground with the issue of unconstitutionality. The charge was not without substance, as Article IX Section 11 of Iowa's constitution declares clearly that "The State University shall be established at one place without branches at any other place, and the university funds shall be applied to that institution and no other." For some critics, this plainly prohibited a second state university in Ames, and those critics included no less a legal authority than SUI Law College Dean Mason Ladd. At one point Ladd wrote President Hancher, arguing that Iowa State University would violate the state constitution—yet for all of his own misgivings about a second public university, Hancher remained quiet on this issue.[23] Iowa State argued that the passage in question had been effectively repealed by Article IX Section 15, which superseded all of the preceding sections. As Hancher was himself a highly qualified legal scholar, his silence suggests that he supported this interpretation, as does the fact that he had already hinted at converting other colleges into "branches" of the State University.

On constitutional questions, of course, scholarly argument does not always trump stubborn popular belief. Plain old-fashioned stubbornness was in fact likely to prove Iowa State's biggest challenge of all. Its alumni, students, faculty and administrators might be united in regarding change as essential, but as a public institution it still required the approval of multiple other authorities. First Hilton would need to get a new name onto the Board of Regents' agenda, then persuade the Regents themselves, then pass through all the machinery of two legislative bodies, and finally obtain the signature of the same governor who remained suspicious that duplication was needlessly driving up education's costs... What now appears inevitable must have seemed, at the time, far from certain.

CHAPTER SIX
A Matter of Identity

The arguments of Iowa State College for changing its name are clear, consistent, and extensively documented in university archives. Arguments against its proposal are nearly as clear, if their documentation is somewhat more diffuse. The ultimate result is beyond question. The full details of how the interested parties arrived at that result, however, are frequently more murky.

At least three historians of Iowa State and its administrators[1] declare that under President Hancher's leadership, State University of Iowa lobbied aggressively against the proposed name-change. President Hilton supported this version of events, writing in his memoir that "it was a very difficult battle to get this change made because of the strenuous objections of people from the State University of Iowa."[2] Hancher certainly objected to the proposal, and remained resentful of it years later.[3] Yet I have found negligible direct evidence of his voicing those objections—in sharp contrast to Hancher's many other critiques of Iowa State. As a result, it's difficult to dismiss the very different narrative of *The University of Iowa in the 20th Century*. According to its author Stow Persons, the Board of Regents, "fearing that open conflict would jeopardize good will to the detriment of both institutions, pressured Hancher not to resist Hilton's drive to change the name of the college to Iowa State University," upon which "Hancher reluctantly agreed..."[4]

Minutes of a March 1959 meeting of the Regents institutions' presidents and provosts only muddy these waters.[5] The bare summary notes, of Iowa State's proposal, only that "A great many questions were raised concerning the move." By this point Hilton had brought his proposal before the board itself already, only to propose that they defer a decision; instead, the board enacted an odd half-a-loaf measure to relabel Iowa State's divisions as colleges while leaving the whole institution still a college, itself.[6] Just days later the presidents and provosts confirmed that they would pursue the larger question again in April.

It's at least possible to see a strategy, in this progress-by-stages approach. Hilton encouraged the board to take extra time to study a file he had provided. I can't help suspecting a further intent that converting Iowa State's colleges to divisions would provide momentum for his greater agenda, and reassurance that the sky would not fall in response to change. In contrast, it's difficult even to guess what might explain President Hancher's actions at the presidents and provosts meeting. After doubtlessly joining in the "many questions" about Iowa State's proposal, Hancher reserved his own item on the April agenda to recommend "a change in the name of the institu-

A MATTER OF IDENTITY

tion at Iowa City if he deems such advisable."[7] Hancher never followed through on any plan to rename State University of Iowa, and to most appearances firmly disapproved of the idea. Though Hancher may not have seen a constitutional issue with renaming Iowa State, he did regard the constitution as prohibiting such a change at SUI, according to one of his successors as president.[8]

Perhaps the only safe conclusion, about Hancher's role, is that he did not care for Iowa State's proposal but felt frustrated by the Board of Regents. His frustration may have been a response to direct warning, as Persons claimed; on the other hand such an intervention may have seemed unnecessary. When the Regents approved Hilton's proposal and recommended it to the legislature, at meetings on April 9 and 10, that may have seemed message enough.

After the Regents' approval, Iowa's legislature was the next official stop for advocates and opponents of changing Iowa State's name. Meanwhile, however, the fight also spread into the informal arena of public opinion. There, concern for maintaining unity or good will was certainly not always a constraint.

The Humboldt Republican was likely the most outspoken opponent of renaming Iowa State College. In two peppery editorials, it voiced many of President Hancher's misgivings, insisting that "We have one University in Iowa" and should not create more. The *Republican* also echoed the accusation of faddism at Iowa State, writing that "It used to be called 'Ames' ... The name 'Ames' was known across the nation because of its educational excellence. Then some aesthetic individual thought 'Ames' was not the proper designation for a good school and began a campaign to have the name changed."⁹

It might be questioned whether or not opponents' cause was ultimately helped by the editorials' curmudgeonly tone, which almost feels less an endorsement of Hancher's views than a satire of them. On the issue of faculty and prestige, the *Republican*'s editors essentially complained that the claim doesn't make sense to them and therefore can't be valid.[10] The paper's views on confusion may have been even less helpful to its cause: "Better leave a good thing alone. As it is now, it is easy to designate 'Iowa State' and 'Iowa University.' [*sic*] That's the common terminology and it is easy to use without confusion."[11]

Other newspapers offered Iowa State more support, if not always with enthusiasm. The *Northwood Anchor* limited its approval to "Okay," and "might as well." But it did approve of Hilton's argument that a new name would help ISC compete for good faculty, and of the view that other states were not baffled by State Universities and therefore Iowans would manage as well.[12] The *Cedar Rapids Gazette* offered a much more ringing endorsement, declaring even before the Regents' meeting that "It's time that the Board of Regents or the state legislature, whichever has jurisdiction, takes action on changing the name of Iowa State college to Iowa State University." The *Gazette*—based little more than 20 miles from Iowa City—urged state leaders to set aside rivalry. "In these days when Iowa is making so much effort to promote the state," wrote its editors, "let's capitalize on one of our really great assets."[13]

President Hilton was certainly pleased to read the *Gazette*'s proclamation, which remains among his papers. But the weeks which followed brought less-encouraging words from the press, and the most worrying appeared outside the op-ed pages. The day after the Regents' vote, the *Ames Tribune* itself warned that "An informal poll Friday indicates the measure may run into trouble in the Iowa Senate." Of 38 senators polled, the *Tribune* reported that only 16 declared themselves in favor of "Iowa State University," with seven undecided and 15 planning to vote against. Journalists had not polled the House, which would vote first and was likely to approve Iowa State's proposal. Yet it seemed in some doubt that the Senate would even consider the measure. Leadership of both parties numbered among its opponents, including Democrats' floor leader, the invariably vocal George O'Malley. According to the *Tribune*, by encouraging the Regents to move slowly President Hilton may have left Senators feeling rushed and irritated: "Several of the legislators expressed comment about the timing of the proposal. 'Why do the regents come up with these recommendations this late in the session?' one asked."[14]

Other newspapers agreed with the *Tribune*'s forecast[15], as did at least one Senate insider. Writing to Hilton soon after the informal poll of his colleagues, Senator Gene L. Hoffman suggested that its results represented a genuine challenge. Hoffman predicted that "We are going to have to do a tremendous job of selling to get this through the legislature."[16]

In the end Hilton and his allies prevailed, but the victory's margin may have come as a surprise. As predicted, the House approved the new name first with minimal fuss. One member voiced concerns about confusion, and tried to reintroduce

"Ames University" as an alternative; rather than risk a distraction by offering any of President Hilton's arguments against the idea, Ames's own representative Ray Cunningham simply replied that "Iowa turned that corner in 1928."[17]

In the Senate, however, concerns were less easily swept aside. Senators ultimately rejected the House legislation, instead taking up an amended version which insisted that a new name for Iowa State would not have any further significance. The amendment declared that "Iowa State University of Science and Technology" would maintain the curriculum and educational policies of Iowa State College of Agriculture and Mechanic Arts, and affirmed that none of the Regents institutions could introduce such changes without approval by the board. The Senator for Ames, Carl Ringgenberg, protested that the added language was superfluous and would merely "fill the code with useless words."[18] But his colleagues remained firm. This was to be their price. Hilton, likely recognizing that opposing the amendment would only inflame the suspicions behind it, gave his assent. It was, he said, "not a problem."[19]

Several months later, Hilton may have had second thoughts about that judgment. For now, though, his calculation of when to push and when to back off produced a most gratifying result: on May 4, 1959, the Iowa Senate voted unanimously to approve Iowa State's new name. Combined with a 96-2 vote when the amended bill returned to the House, the outcome was nothing short of a triumph. Whatever lobbying State University of Iowa may or may not have conducted in opposition, Hilton had certainly worked hard to win over the Senate. Looking back afterward, he chalked up the conversion of perhaps two dozen "no" votes to "the help of a number of senators and intensive personal conferences with every member."[20] His intervention paid off. If the governor's approval had been in any doubt, overwhelming support by the General Assembly seemed to settle the issue. Within a week of the second House vote, Governor Loveless signed the final bill. The student-run *Daily* declared at once: "It's Iowa State University."[21]

Technically this was premature. Iowa State College continued to exist until a default effective date for Iowa legislation of July 4. In any event, fully implementing the change was certain to take several months and perhaps years. As administrator "Dutch" Elder commented, the old name was everywhere on campus and replacing it was a literally monumental task; "'Iowa State College' must be engraved an inch deep in the front of the [Beardshear] building," he noted.[22]

Iowa State was happy enough to take on the challenge. Elsewhere, discontent with its new name persisted years after lawmakers' thumbs-up. In 1964 a Westphalia, Iowa, grade school student wrote Hilton, after examining the Iowa Constitution in history class and concluding that Iowa State University appeared to be in violation of Article IX Section 11.[23] The president passed the letter to an assistant who sent a polite, detailed reply.[24] When a secretary for the SUI sociology department named Mildred Beem wrote in 1962, by contrast, Hilton may only have filed her suggestion to "request that your university be renamed AMES UNIVERSITY, AMES, IOWA."[25] Beem reported receiving several letters meant for Iowa State every week, along with occasional books and other parcels. Her situation was not unique, either, as reported in a news clipping in the same file. Postmasters and campus mail offices encountered misdirected mail dozens of times per day.[26]

Newspapers were tripping up, as well. If none of these phenomena were new, the result fell well short of assurances that Iowa would face no issues with confusion.

Having invested great effort in one change of name, however, President Hilton was not volunteering his institution for another. President Hancher shared the vexation of his sociology department's secretary, but he too declined to offer suggestions. The obvious alternative was, as more than one newspaper suggested, "a striking out of 'State' from the name of the University of Iowa."[27] Yet general opinion also agreed that this would require amending the state constitution. Hancher's own suggested outcome, meanwhile, had been resolutely ignored by the Board of Regents. It's tempting to imagine a bitter satisfaction in the SUI president's modest request of the Regents, some time later, that they look into solutions. *You made this mess, you fix it*, he might have implied with every justification.

Amid all of the drama and consternation, however, at least a few observers managed to recognize an element of humor. Disappointed SUI partisans, in particular, might have appreciated a suggestion of the *Sioux Center News* following the legislature's approval of renaming Iowa State. Mocking the months of protests about prestige, and scholarly breadth, it reported that "Already, the 'university' has a new nick-name—Moo-U."[28] This was a decent early effort; personally, however, I think the *Winterset Madisonian* took the prize a few months later: "they used to call Iowa State the 'Cow college.' Now they call it 'the udder university.'"[29]

CHAPTER SEVEN
Marking Territory

Iowa State University's historians have ascribed some remarkable things to President Virgil Hancher. He campaigned against the school changing its name. He fought Iowa State's admission to the Association of American Universities. He personally hated President Hilton. I found each of these suggestions remarkable, at any rate, and I will presume that most who read this far share at least some of that interest. Of all Hancher's purported aggressions, though, none surprised me more than the claim that he vigorously opposed Iowa State offering degrees in English and speech. This seemed such petty, vindictive animosity as to be grotesque, in a way that exceeded any of Hancher's other objections. Yet it is more reliably documented than almost all of the others.

Unlike Iowa State's new name, or its candidacy for the AAU, President Hancher made his objections to an ISU major in English repeatedly, and publicly, leaving behind an ample paper trail. He also went into deep detail about his reasoning, which does at all events challenge the notion of a simple reactionary turf battle. He found powerful allies, too—though at the same time he was so vocal that a number of State University of Iowa's own alumni called on him to back down. Hancher never did so willingly, and even after giving his arguments their full due, his lasting offense at this particular proposal can appear excessive. Seemingly here, if anywhere, is indisputable evidence of arrogant "big brother" selfishly trying to hold back "little brother." The basic facts are beyond dispute.

Unfortunately for this version of events, there are more facts that tell a larger story. In that story Hancher's SUI may still be a bully but it isn't the only one, or even the first. Well before Hancher entertained even a single unkind thought about James Hilton, the Iowa State president's administration was picking on "littler brother" Iowa State Teachers College. Most awkward of all, it was doing so in exactly the same way.

In fairness to President James Hilton, he largely walked into Iowa State's efforts to restrict curriculum at ISTC after they had begun. He also did nothing in particular to stop them. Presumably he could have, even if it would have been difficult saying no to Helen LeBaron. Just beginning an eventual long career running Iowa State's home economics programs, LeBaron was a human dynamo who also squeezed in endless volunteer work, boards of directors, national committee appointments and several years on the Ames City Council. Being a woman dedicating her career to domestic arts in the 1950s did not dissuade her from forming strong opinions and fighting for them. One month before Hilton took office as president, she wrote Iowa State's dean of science Harold Gaskill to express her very negative opinion of a proposed new course at ISTC.

That Iowa State Teachers College earned LeBaron's ire by proposing to teach vocational home economics may surpass any other example of how obscure the era's conflicts now appear, in their details. In 2015, home economics is essentially a minor program at Iowa State University. Promoted to a college along with other divisions in 1959, it was renamed the College of Family and Consumer Sciences in 1987, then merged with the College of Education in 2005 under the heading "Human Sciences." Long before that, the distinction between home economics and vocational home economics was already fine. A contemporary newspaper article suggested that "The difference between a vocational home economics teacher and other home economics teachers is largely one of federal definitions."[1] Today the very term is nearly obsolete.

In 1953, however, Helen LeBaron was dean of a full-fledged college of home economics (even if it was not formally labeled a college) and took all of its offerings very seriously. Writing to Gaskill, she argued that Iowa State should firmly oppose ISTC establishing a rival program in vocational home economics. First, she wrote, it would violate the Board of Education's edict against duplication. Second, it would distract ISTC from a more basic responsibility that was already being neglected; LeBaron asserted that nearly one-third of Iowa high schools lacked certified teachers of general homemaking, and suggested that ISTC would do better to focus more on this subject, which it already offered. As a teachers college, LeBaron added, ISTC was better suited than Iowa State to prepare these teachers, whom high schools frequently assigned additional subjects. Finally, LeBaron protested that a duplicate vocational home economics program would harm the high quality and standing of home economics at Iowa State. Declaring that "we have an unusually fine faculty with a large proportion holding doctor's degrees," she warned that a competing ISTC program would inevitably divert resources from Iowa State and result in loss of top faculty.[2]

Short of actually employing the word "mediocrity," LeBaron's complaints prefigured many of President Hancher's later themes to an uncanny degree. Details of the competition for funding were somewhat different, here; LeBaron was particularly concerned about federal grants for vocational education in home economics and other subjects. But in general she made most of the same arguments later offered by the Hancher administration: *the Board charges us to avoid duplication, Iowa's schools should focus on established specialties, a competing department will dilute the budget and prestige of our own.* While Hilton himself had little to say, Iowa State pressed these objections throughout his first year, and as president he was ultimately responsible. His administration's response to the Budget and Financial Control Committee in 1954 took a very aggressive line on duplication in general: "If constant vigilance in this respect is not maintained, many departments tend to expand their offerings to the point where they are actually conducting parallel courses under different names."[3]

The arguments deployed by Iowa State Teachers College and its president, in response, offer interest as well. Notably, President Maucker made a case for prestige's value in attracting good faculty five years before Hilton offered the same rationale for changing Iowa State's title from college to university. A memo to the Board of Education suggested, in favor of ISTC's proposal, that "Restriction against preparing teachers for vocational home making is interpreted by many as indication of a low caliber program" and was prompting both prospective students and faculty to look elsewhere.[4] The proposed program, Maucker told the Board, would allow ISTC "to strengthen our instructional program without appreciable additional cost."[5]

Beyond this, the Teachers College played down the idea that its program would pose any competition to Iowa State's. In addition to ceding any claim to the federal grants that concerned LeBaron, ISTC's dean of faculty suggested that "I suspect that the Iowa State people are not so well acquainted with our relatively small set-up" and might be reassured by touring the modest programs in Cedar Falls.[6] Maucker's administration also pointed to existing duplication within areas that were arguably its own area of responsibility, noting for example that "All three institutions have prepared persons for careers in public schools during most of the lives of the institutions."[7] Above all, the ISTC president questioned whether the Board's formal aversion to duplication should really restrain the development of Iowa higher education at all times, and in all places. "Duplication has almost come to be a 'scare word,'" he wrote as the Board weighed a final decision in early 1955. Previewing his later thoughts on appropriate "Future Directions" for Iowa's colleges, he asserted that "Not all duplication is bad; in fact, some duplication is both necessary and desirable."[8]

For interpreting the larger battles over curriculum between Iowa State and State University of Iowa that followed, however, the most significant feature of the skirmish over vocational home economics is its outcome. In May 1955, the Board voted to approve the ISTC proposal. While remaining formally in favor of three distinct institutions and opposed to further duplication, it chose to respect President Maucker's arguments for making an exception. I can only guess that Dean LeBaron did not welcome this outcome. Though President Hilton's papers record no direct comments on the issue, it may be that he was disappointed as well. I have a stronger suspicion that, whatever his opinion of Maucker's reasoning or the Board's response, he was certainly paying attention to both.

By autumn of 1959, James Hilton had already been through a very full year even for a university president. He had parried proposed restrictions on "Future Directions" for his institution, with a detailed, forceful response. He had, through intense personal conferences, won over more than a dozen state senators to recognizing Iowa State as a university. He had maintained the ongoing effort to persuade legislators to provide adequate funding. He was overseeing plans to open an experimental two-year technical institute the following year. He was, as always, still trying to scare up resources for the Iowa State Center.

In September, Hilton also earned one of his most memorable anecdotes at the cost of a very tense moment or two. With Cold War tensions relaxing slightly, if still quite high, an eccentric farmer named Roscoe Garst had invited the leader of the Soviet Union to visit Iowa, and premier Nikita Kruschev had accepted. Kruschev spent the morning of September 23 with Garst (who regularly wrote Hilton with various novel suggestions as well) inspecting his farm. While in the area, the premier and his party then spent the afternoon touring Iowa State University. Despite the Cold War and guards from the Secret Service, Hilton recalled Kruschev's manner as ebullient, perhaps even impish. Security arrangements called for keeping curious students at a distance but they repeatedly circumvented this, to Kruschev's delight. Students lined windows of MacKay Hall "while Kruschev was supposedly looking at demonstrations there," Hilton wrote, and "He immediately went to the windows and shook hands with the students... as if he were campaigning for office."[9] Secret Servicemen may have been less amused by this, but they were absolutely frantic when, a little later, a group of unknown persons approached wearing long coats and dark glasses, and carrying violin cases.

Just moments later the grim faces split with amusement. A handful of students had decided it would be funny to give the Soviet premier and the Secret Service a scare. Kruschev, doubtless to the great relief of his hosts, agreed; in Hilton's words, after explanations were made the premier "was very amused and slapped his knee as he laughed heartily." Years later, Hilton acknowledged the incident among other amusing moments of his presidency. All the same, he confessed, in most cases "They were not so amusing at the time."[10]

Under the circumstances, President Hilton might have decided that he had taken on enough for 1959. The Regents had tasked Iowa State and the other schools with hammering out development plans—this had first prompted the "Future Directions" argument earlier in the year—but there are always means of deferring bureaucratic chores of this type. Hilton might very reasonably have employed them to focus on other work, or even to take an afternoon to unwind. Courtesy of coach Clay Stapleton, Cyclone football was finally winning games. Reduced to just 30 healthy players, the team that finished a victory over Drake University covered in mud became a minor legend as the "Dirty 30."[11]

But while President Hilton enjoyed a rousing gridiron contest or other diversions, when he allowed himself the time, these were not the reasons he had returned to Iowa State. In his first address to staff, he had pledged not only to fight the school's battles but to fight for specific, additional development beyond existing programs. As much as Hilton revered Iowa State's achievements in agriculture, home economics, or other applied sciences he had concluded that deeper responsibilities to society demanded more. In 1953 he declared "…we must train citizens who will have some understanding of the great moral and social issues of our day. We must have more research and education in social sciences and in human relationships because herein lie some of the greatest problems of our times."[12] Six years later, he remained as convinced of this as ever, and meanwhile the Board of Regents was asking him to outline plans for his university. The time had come, and Hilton was not going to be diverted by other projects or deterred by the already contentious year behind him. He would deliver his views on developing Iowa State University, and its peers as well.

On its face, President Hilton's 1959 plan for expanded humanities and social sciences at Iowa State was simple. He wanted to introduce degree-granting majors in English and speech, and modern languages. He later added physical education for women to this list, but with or without this addition it seems a very modest request relative to the great controversy that resulted.

Hilton's arguments could be judged straightforward as well, given that most of them had been advanced by Iowa State Teachers College six years earlier, and judged adequate. I hesitate to suggest that Hilton lifted material directly from ISTC and President Maucker; an idea is rare indeed that has no precedent elsewhere, and quite possibly both Maucker and Hilton were already familiar with similar reasoning before the debate over vocational home economics. But whatever the platform's origin it had obviously persuaded the Board of Regents just a few years earlier. Hilton can have seen no compelling reason to depart from the same script, and he did not do so. He repeated the suggestion that good faculty valued having students majoring in their field, emphasizing that restricting them to service-course roles was not thrift but rather increasingly costly. Iowa State spent more than most schools to attract equally qualified English and speech faculty, yet department morale was low, turnover was high, and quality suffered.[13] Just like Maucker and ISTC, Hilton insisted that Iowa State's programs would be very modest. The department would remain small. He was asking for neither master's degrees nor PhDs.[14] His provost James Jensen explicitly declared that "the 'main show' in these fields will be recognized as being at the University in Iowa City."[15]

President Hilton's other arguments were generally simple and direct as well. As with his campaign to rename Iowa State, he acknowledged that trends did play a part and ISU could not realistically ignore them. Relevant professional societies were strongly recommending more social science and humanities curricula for students majoring in the sciences. Other land-grant institutions had already responded, and Iowa State, Hilton insisted, "can do no less than this."[16] Already, it was "the only four-year institution in the state of Iowa which does not now offer a major in English."[17] English and speech, and modern languages, were basic disciplines and well within ISU's traditional responsibilities. The closest that President Hilton came to any sort of esoteric argument was in claiming that at Iowa State these majors would emphasize science and technology, producing in effect a different curriculum than the bachelor of arts programs at a liberal arts college.[18]

In contrast, most of President Hancher's reasons for opposing the new majors at Iowa State demanded a more ambitious conceptual reach. As he marshaled his objections to the newest item on Hilton's agenda, Hancher argued again for a holistic view of Iowa higher education instead. If the state had need to expand language programs, in his view the most natural place to do so was at its liberal arts university.[19] Hancher also continued warning that a kind of domino effect would follow from duplication. He proposed that "the pressures for expanding programs into the masters and doctors degrees were natural once undergraduate degrees were established," no matter how sincere Hilton's reassurances at the moment.[20] The ultimate result would be, of course, a complete duplicate liberal arts college, dilution of funds, and mediocrity.

The alternative which Hancher outlined was the most challenging of all his ideas, perhaps in any context. He proposed,

Three Presidents: Virgil M. Hancher, James H. Hilton and J. William Maucker.
University Photographs, Box 62, Iowa State University Library Special Collections.

in effect, transforming the whole prevailing concept of liberal education. Hilton, in order to integrate more humanities into applied science curricula, basically advocated traditional social science and humanities courses with an emphasis on relevance to science; essentially, i.e., to teach liberal arts somewhat more scientifically. Hancher's solution in turn envisioned teaching sciences much more liberally.

Throughout his career President Hancher thought, spoke, and wrote frequently on the issue of liberal education. By 1960, as Iowa State campaigned for majors in English and speech, etc., he had expanded and refined his thesis that this direct approach was a flawed, peculiarly American model. It was still both costly and elaborate in practice, he argued, while simplistic in its thinking: "a liberally educated man is not produced automatically by the study of any particularly designated subject matter. A liberally educated man is one who, by whichever route he has come, has achieved that breadth of outlook and depth of wisdom which enable him to see life steadily and to see it whole." Simply assigning students social sciences or humanities requirements, Hancher believed, might only provide a liberal education on paper. "Too often his liberal courses seem an obstacle to be overcome in order to get on with the professional study which is his goal," he warned.[21]

For his own solution Hancher turned back once more to his studies at Oxford. In his case, studying the history of Roman and English law as part of his primary coursework had opened his eyes to broader views of society and history in general, and—just as important—to how his chosen profession interacted with them. Hancher called for similar integration of liberalizing knowledge and ideas into American professional and science majors' core curriculum. Warming to his theme, he speculated on the likely product of Hilton's approach:

> The engineer is not made a liberally educated man merely by adding Chaucer to Engineering Drawing. ... Indeed if the engineer learns his Chaucer only because it is an obstacle to be overcome, he may well end up by becoming a pedant both in Chaucer and in Engineering Drawing. On the other hand, if his Engineering Drawing is so taught that it opens his eyes to the civilizations it has served and to the social utility out of which it has come, how can he escape becoming a more liberally educated man?[22]

MARKING TERRITORY

Again Hancher took an instinctively holistic view. Think beyond assembly-line curriculum models, he urged, think beyond trying to solve every institution's problems within that institution, think beyond the way things happen to be done in our culture and look further afield. It was heady stuff, admirable for a leader of higher education. It was also, however, an awkward pitch to offer the bureaucratic system that was the presidents' most important audience. Hancher's own ideas were complex, in their demand for imagination and different perspectives. The complexity which he also perceived in Hilton's approach was, however, the sort with which bureaucracy is most comfortable; if it was in some sense elaborate it could be diagrammed, and if it was costly the costs could be calculated with formulae.

For the Board of Regents, then, President Hilton's request was at least straightforward in and of itself. But Hilton was making that request within a larger context. In that fuller context his pursuit of this modest, simple proposal led onto narrow, tricky paths.

At the same time that Iowa State was defending its right to introduce new majors, it was still campaigning against one of its peers doing exactly the same thing. While President Hancher spoke in favor of larger, grander visions, his administration had also replied to the Regents with more immediate and concrete proposals. In combination with reactions from ISU, these State University of Iowa requests challenge any impression of a simple or straightforward conflict.

Hancher's provost Harvey Davis suggested several new SUI majors, over the course of 1959. Two in particular might almost have been chosen to cast Hilton and Iowa State in an awkward light: vocational home economics, and nuclear engineering. The request for vocational home economics, of course, reminded one and all that Hilton's presidency had previously resisted much the same case that it was now arguing for itself. One of Davis's memos is remarkably frank in emphasizing this very point. Declaring it "highly important" that SUI introduce a vocational home economics major, he adds that "I hardly need to list arguments here for they are essentially the same as those listed by Dr. Maucker..."[23]

The SUI provost's case for nuclear engineering seems to have been, initially, even more an overt criticism of Iowa State's positions. At the early 1959 meeting when President Hilton and his own provost first made their pitch for extending social sciences and humanities offerings, Davis seems to have selected nuclear engineering simply as a hypothetical counter-example, i.e. *well, what about this?* He pointed out that SUI could present similar justifications for adding new degrees, asserting that "a number of extremely competent men on the University staff feel that the University must offer a major in nuclear engineering." Yet, he added, the major would still violate Regents policies.[24]

The SUI proposal for nuclear engineering illustrates as well as anything how complex the curriculum debates became for all participants. In the months that followed his rhetorical suggestion, Davis repeated it as an increasingly serious proposal. By autumn he formally included it along with his request for vocational home economics.[25] Meanwhile, in elaborating on his justification for the degree, he turned yet another of Iowa State's arguments back on President Hilton. The "new" major in English and speech, Hilton maintained, could be provided without any new staff or other resources; ISU's existing departments needed only permission. Pressing for nuclear engineering degrees, Davis wrote that "We have the courses now... Our staff feels that there would be considerable gain in allowing these courses to be grouped together to form a major."[26]

If Hilton appreciated the contradictions in his position, however, he was unembarrassed by them. His administration continued to oppose duplication in vocational home economics, as well as the proposed nuclear engineering major. In late 1959 Iowa State circulated a memo responding to all of SUI's proposals for expanded curriculum to that point. Its comments are a mix of polite approval and mulish obstinacy, plus what seems like yet another example of gratuitous needling.

On both vocational home economics and nuclear engineering, the Hilton administration remained inflexible. It claimed that both fell within the preserve of Iowa State, and should remain reserved for it as neither was a basic discipline like English and speech. (The already enacted extension of vocational home economics to Iowa State Teachers College went unmentioned, perhaps for multiple reasons.) Nuclear engineering, in contrast, required extremely expensive infrastructure, and while SUI already offered and ought to offer some courses in the subject, they could not be combined into a full-fledged major as simply as Davis had suggested.

Some of this is an awkward fit with Hilton's general arguments, elsewhere, but with allowance for nuance it's at least reasonable. The ISU memo reinforces this appearance with positive comments on a number of other proposed degrees. It declares a master's in library science plainly needed, for example, adding that "Iowa State enthusiastically supports this proposal." An urban and regional planning program also receives favor, despite ISU reporting both plans and resources for expansion in the same area; "in our judgment," the memo asserts "this is an area in which the efforts of both Iowa State and SUI are needed."[27]

Responding to several proposed PhDs, Hilton's administration affirmed that it had no objections to any. If a relatively lukewarm endorsement, this might still have amounted to a demonstration of the support Iowa State wanted for its own proposals—except that ISU seemed unable to leave things there. The memo appends "a friendly suggestion from a sister institution" that gerontology, public administration and social psychology were, in its authors' view, excessively "narrow and fragmented Ph.D. programs."[28] As ever, sincerity seems the safest assumption absent firm evidence to the contrary. Whatever its intent, however, my instinct is that the recipients of this friendly suggestion may have seen it as more than a little obnoxious.

By their last phase, arguments over curriculum proposals took on a fractious character unmistakable even in half-century-old papers. In April 1960, Harvey Davis offered to support Iowa State Teachers College granting bachelor of arts degrees without teacher certification, if President Maucker would limit participation to 100 students. Whether or not Davis was baiting the president, he provoked an angry reaction. "Maucker immediately took exception to that," reported the *Ames Tribune*, "and said his reasons for asking for the current expansion were 'not merely to educate a few pupils who happen to wander onto the campus by mistake. We are seeking approval of a major step in the evolution of the institute (at Cedar Falls),' Maucker said."[29] This, of course, may have been Davis's very point. But even the pretense of a shared antipathy to duplication was cracking under strain, now.

Newspapers picked up on this tension, and drew in new acrimony from outside the Regents bureaucracy. Less than two weeks later the *Tribune* published an open letter from 10 SUI alumni who had also completed degrees at Iowa State. They had learned of President Hancher's opposition to an ISU English degree, and wanted both Hancher and the general public to hear their disapproval. "As State University of Iowa alums," they wrote, "we are shocked that you, as president of a great educational institution, would oppose Iowa State's request for these majors." The letter repeated most of Hilton's talking points—faculty morale, no extra cost, a major in English at nearly every peer school already—combined with an overt attempt to shame Hancher for pettiness. Insisting that "There is room for two very good universities in Iowa," the alumni admonished that "Your endorsement of these major courses at Iowa State University will go a long way in gaining this end."[30] Hancher would not believe it, and might have pointed out that Iowa State's own "room for all" policy was very selective. Yet he was being lectured in public while Hilton seemed to receive a pass.

In private, though, the situation was very different. At the end of April Hilton's office issued a press release to address "misunderstanding and confusion" about its requested majors.[31] It was essentially a summary of points that Hilton had already made, many times. But the points chosen for re-emphasis had a notably defensive theme. Iowa State was not establishing a liberal arts college; it was not changing its direction or emphasis; the new degrees would include a distinctive science orientation, etc. Had President Hancher noted the news release he might have suspected that Hilton was, in fact, getting his own share of sharp criticism. He would have been right, too.

Iowa State historian Dorothy Schweider suggested that Hilton "had to walk something of a tightrope in stating Iowa State's need for... humanities and social sciences while always de-emphasizing their importance."[32] These were certainly difficult messages to balance, and at times Hilton slipped. At least three Iowa senators wrote the president in April 1960, just as indignant as the 10 SUI alumni. Replying to Senator W.C. Stuart, Hilton acknowledged a belief "that the requests are in violation of some of the statements I made to some of the members of the 58th General Assembly."[33] Before that same General Assembly, Hilton had reacted calmly to the amendment insisting Iowa State would not change direction along with its name. It was, he had assured lawmakers, "not a problem." Now, though, it was coming back to haunt him.

Hilton tried to play down the significance of the same majors that he was, obviously, trying very hard to secure. He played up distinctive emphases planned at Iowa State and suggested that these would, furthermore, ensure the programs in question remained small. "The rigor of the proposed majors... heavily loaded as they will be with maths and science courses, and wholly unlike the background demanded in the traditional liberal arts institutions, will discourage very many students to [sic] take majors in these fields," he wrote Senator Irving Long, repeating the protest in his letter to Stuart.[34]

In answering Senator Robert Rigler, the usually measured Hilton was so exasperated as to begin one sentence "For the life of me…"[35] Eager to perform damage control, he foreswore any interest in library science, law or medicine. As a final argument in his defense, Hilton suggested that his critics were a minority view and that he had received far more positive comments on balance. Still, the negative letters were jarring to the same James Hilton who had been showered with favor by North Carolina's lawmakers, and who had more recently won unanimous consent from Iowa's senate for ISU's new name. Being accused of betrayal, even by a few legislators, likely stung Hilton much more than a public rebuke from alumni upset Virgil Hancher.

With large ambitions for ISU still unfulfilled, President Hilton had good reason to show concern over any rupture with lawmakers. For the time being, though, he needn't have worried. Trends were running in favor of growing Iowa's public colleges. Enrollments were rising and likely to rise for many years. The Board of Regents had ignored Iowa State's protests and approved vocational home economics at Iowa State Teachers College several years earlier, and had in turn formally made Iowa State a second university over President Hancher's objections more recently. The original prompt for the latest battles suggested, by itself, that President Maucker's view of duplication as simply a "scare word" was making gains. Where past boards had drawn up detailed plans to impose program cuts from above, the newest Regents had asked schools to coordinate development and growth, among themselves.

The end result was opposition to very little, except opposition itself. Despite all the complaints from ISU, the board blessed vocational home economics and nuclear engineering at State University of Iowa, though SUI had to wait somewhat longer. The Regents approved Hilton's requests in May 1960, while recent acrimony was still fresh; the board itself split on all of Iowa State's new degrees except physical education for women. Still, President Hilton could be satisfied with the outcome. If he would have preferred to keep a few programs exclusive to Iowa State, when push came to shove he was more concerned with rounding out his institution than with constraining his peers'. When promising staff that he would fight, he also warned that he would not win every battle.[36] He could, however, report again that he had won those which mattered most.

President Hancher could take no such consolation. Even in winning, eventually, contested majors in vocational home economics and nuclear engineering, he had lost the larger argument. A few months after the dust settled, in August 1960 he spoke at the University of Wisconsin School of Banking in Madison, on "Some Problems of Higher Education." The president began by setting out all of his familiar complaints, as fervently as ever. He posited "a curious law of institutional growth at work—one worthy of study by sociologists—which says: Plant a special purpose educational institution and you reap a university." Land-grant colleges had been lured to discard their distinctive purpose, he insisted with considerable bitterness: "The once proud words 'agriculture and mechanic arts,' have either been dropped from their titles or from their fields of emphasis, except for the umbilical cord which ties these institutions to the federal treasury."[37] Teachers colleges were going the same way, and it seemed likely to Hancher that the new junior colleges would be applying for university status themselves within 50 years.

Next he repeated once more his alternative concept, of integrating liberal education into applied science and professional curricula. After years of polish, it was possibly the most eloquent and accessible version of the ideas that he ever composed. Yet as he acknowledged, it seemed in vain. It demanded an openness to new theories, as well as a quality of teacher training, that were in both cases unlikely to emerge from prevailing practices. Having repeated the beliefs he had consistently advocated for years, and affirmed his certainty of their truth, Hancher conceded that he had failed to convince others. If there remained any consolation at all, it was that the situation was a recognized part of life for an old lawyer. His bitterness and disappointment spent, Hancher left his audience with a glimmer of humor:

> When I was a member of the Law Club of Chicago there used to be a saying that The Law Club was a forum in which the program speaker for the evening reargued the case which he had lost in the courts. If there are university faculty or administrative officers present tonight, they will recognize the analogy and will know what I mean.[38]

CHAPTER EIGHT
Halftime

One of my favorite stories about Virgil Hancher connects up a number of traits that characterized him as person, and as president. I think that it offers an especially useful vignette of the differences between Hancher and James Hilton. The centrality of a student automobile to the story is a mild irony, for that reason; cars on campus may have been the subject on which the two presidents could sympathize most completely. Hilton lamented the number of student-owned cars clogging Iowa State's campus in one of his first convocation speeches,[1] and remained vexed by the problem in his last, more than a decade later.[2] Hancher reflected that the sound of squealing tires alerted him to the start of Rush Week more reliably than a calendar—and that even aggressive braking failed to stop more than one errant car from crashing through the hedge bordering his home.

One incident stood out in the president's recollection, however, as recorded in a sketch biography:

HANCHER VS. HILTON

There was a day some years ago when a student-piloted car almost ran him down at the Madison-Washington street intersection, opposite the Library. The president jotted down the license number, and the car's owner was called to his office.

The young man arrived at the appointed hour, brightly polished and neatly groomed, as one expecting a citation.

"Do you recall driving down the Washington street hill yesterday afternoon and almost striking a pedestrian at the bottom?" asked the President.

To the student's eyes came the light of recollection. "Yes, I do," he said. "Actually, my roommate was driving at the time, but I remember telling him to watch out for that old coot at the curb."

"I," began the president briskly, "am that old coot."[3]

Here is the brilliant student and successful lawyer—erudite, precise, and witty at once—yet ultimately something of a fish out of water. Both the story and the side of Hancher that it captures delight me. Perceptive and well-educated, Hancher did not suffer fools gladly, and the fact that life constantly required this of him was, I suspect, an ongoing affront to his basic dignity. Nonetheless he could find enormous patience and even an acerbic humor in responding. Having been nearly flattened by what might have been blithe, blundering ignorance incarnate, Hancher did not chase afterward or rage in place, or yell for police. Instead, he calmly organized his evidence. Then he interrogated his unwitting suspect politely, even gently—Hancher's careful approach proving well advised when he learned that this was not his main target—only to spring a trap the moment his interviewee walked into it, while still betraying no more than a hint of his annoyance. This as much as anything endears Hancher to me, despite all of his quarrels with my alma mater. Unfortunately for President Hancher, I suspect that the very same habits won him rather less favor in pursuing those quarrels.

President Hilton might have handled the above circumstance differently from Hancher, or he may have handled it exactly the same. I can say with confidence, however, that his style in general was very different. Everything about Hancher suggests a figure of authority, convinced of his argument as well as his qualifications, telling an audience what he has concluded and counting on them to recognize its truth. He trained as a scholar and lawyer, and before that excelled at debate. Even visually, Hancher looked like a commanding presence. In photos from his early presidency Hancher seems almost inappropriately young, but with features still approaching a leading-man quality. As years passed they etched an image of dignity and wisdom; in maturity Hancher might have been the image of some great Roman orator he had studied at Oxford.

James Hilton was a much less compelling figure, at first glance. Earlier in adulthood he looked like an amiable good old boy, of perhaps modest talents but no great distinction. As age wore away his hair and rounded off his features, he began to look like no one at all, an anonymous face in the crowd behind steel-rimmed 1950s glasses. Hilton's temperament was similarly unsuited to enthralling a large audience. His own student debate efforts were unmemorable, like much of his academic career, and if he ultimately achieved a PhD and high office they did not result in the style of an authority. Minutes of one meeting of presidents and provosts note that Hilton

Virgil M. Hancher, c. 1960.
F.W. Kent Collection, University Archives, The University of Iowa Libraries.

HALFTIME

"read a statement" of his positions,[4] and I can only imagine that Hancher would have been unimpressed. He would have spoken extempore, or at least memorized his remarks; on such occasions as he did speak from notes, hand-marked pauses and emphases make it clear that he was still speaking rather than reading.

Those same rhetorical abilities that served Hancher so well as debate champion or lawyer, however, may have been more hindrance than help as president of a public university. The late historian Stow Persons described Hancher as remote from his faculty and staff, more interested in directing than leading.[5] Persons's years as part of that faculty may support his assessment or they may reflect a grudge, but Hancher's style and manner are certainly compatible with the suggestion. As are Hancher's results with other audiences which he could not compel, but only try to persuade. Making his case for greater appropriations in early 1961, Hancher referred to a decline in American prestige and so offended two lawmakers' patriotism that they threatened to cut his budget instead.[6] The episode proved mostly bluster, but legislators' threats were not always so empty. Even when Hancher avoided offense, moreover, he struggled to win converts from the statehouse, the Regents, or his colleagues. Whatever the specifics involved, I have a suspicion that none of those groups enjoyed being lectured.

Hilton, for all his limitations as a formal speaker, did not lecture. As much as possible he did not attempt to be a formal speaker, at all, but rather to listen and converse.[7] Contemporary accounts and historians agree that Hilton preferred sitting down and talking one-on-one. His was the approach of a salesman with nothing but the goodwill he could earn, rather than a lawyer with an Oxford degree. James G. Hilton supports historians' conclusion that his father's years as a county extension agent—a role much like that of a salesman—helped him relate to legislators, and I think this must be a large part of any advantage the president had in lobbying.

It's worth drawing a contrast, here, with warmth and charisma, areas where appearances may confound natural assumptions. For all that President Hancher might be assumed to be frosty and condescending, multiple accounts describe him as warm and winning in person, with a gift for telling stories.[8] Hilton seems in other ways the more personable and colorful figure. He was known to chew on cigars, and flashes of a broad grin supply the one recognizable element among younger and older photos—despite which he sometimes left a serious, officious impression even on those who most admired him. He was certainly no bon vivant, and had few interests or hobbies outside of work, even by the standards of a university president.[9]

Nonetheless Hilton was popular with almost everyone, from colleagues to legislators to students.[10] The key to his effectiveness, I think, lay less in likability than in humility. Both he and Hancher grew up on a farm, but Hilton seems to have internalized that origin much more deeply. His longer formal association with agriculture no doubt helped in connecting with rural legislators—just as Hancher had worried in his letter opposing land-grant colleges for AAU membership—but Hilton's more general aura of "a very humble guy"[11] was probably just as appreciated by senators from Dubuque or board members from Des Moines.

HALFTIME

Perhaps just as important, Hilton made his approach a policy as much as a personality. One Iowa lawmaker specifically praised Hilton's respectful approach as a contrast with the Hancher administration's, confiding that "he felt that they were trying to brainwash him when he visited Iowa City."[12] Hilton took very little for granted, ending nearly every speech to faculty or staff all through his presidency with gratitude for their loyalty. He came to Ames with significant ambitions, certainly, but still took time to listen to every constituency before drawing detailed plans. He felt certain that Iowa State College was enough of a university without changing its name, yet he patiently heard out other views rather than explaining why they were wrong; when he changed his mind and began lobbying in favor of a new name, he had the benefit of understanding skeptics' own perspectives.

Just like everyone else Hilton was fallible, of course. Even with favorable relations, he had more success winning approval for programs he could claim as cost-free than for increased funds which he considered at least as important. He also managed to offend valued constituencies from time to time, and could be at least as exasperated with the result as President Hancher. In Hilton's case, this seemed to pass rather than harden into more lasting pessimism, although that may be as much a product of success as its cause. It's still safe to say that Hilton was more in tune with his audiences than Hancher. But it's also worth considering that Hilton was simply more in step with his times.

In some ways, President Hancher probably pursued the wrong types of argument entirely. Despite his holistic vision for a liberal arts curriculum subtly blended in to other disciplines, he seems more often fixated on clearly defined rules and divisions.[13] Each of the Regents schools was supposed to serve a distinct role, the overall system was supposed to avoid duplication, and no one had formally repealed any of these policies—yet he saw rules being bent and boundaries blurred, and protested that this was not right. In a court of law or debating society, it certainly wouldn't be. But the rigid system Hancher was trying to defend was compromised by the mushy realities of politics, and in truth always had been. Iowa's public colleges had not developed from an orderly, coordinated plan. The Board of Education's 1912 attempt to impose one found the board's formal authority completely meaningless, in the face of informal political pressures. Smaller ambiguities abounded before and after; for every law or policy statement Hancher cited, President Hilton could usually find other language amounting to an "elastic clause."

The mismatch of Hancher's policy conservatism with more casual politics grew more severe in the late 1950s, however. Hancher was never insensitive to political pressures, any more than he was entirely unwilling to bend a rule when necessary (as with his administration's disregard for strict pre-auditing). But after nearly 20 years as president, his attitude toward political interaction with higher education was largely negative. In a 1954 speech he warned that "sinister changes are in the making," resulting from lawmakers imposing more and more oversight on higher education policy.[14] After hearings and audits and one injunction after another to curtail expansion, he seemed convinced that quietly respecting established limits and avoiding politicians' notice was the safest course.

For my part I think his conclusions were decidedly reasonable. They simply proved, in retrospect, largely wrong. Swelling enrollment was probably the chief reason. As far back as 1925, one of the board's independent reports suggested that when most colleges were adding more students, the costs of duplicating programs were rarely worth worrying about.[15] Authorities remained suspicious anyway, but as 1960 approached, their stern statements against duplication were beginning to diverge from practical policy. Even before the baby boom's long-anticipated arrival on campus, the proportion of high school graduates applying to college was already growing. In this context, arguments against adding programs or even whole universities inevitably lost some of their force. Hilton could point out that Iowa State was a relative laggard, in seeking university status, and again in applying to introduce an English major. If Iowa's legislators were still slower to fund growth than to approve it, even appropriations began to catch up by Hilton's later years.

It's difficult to argue that President Hancher should have foreseen all of this. Hilton deserves some credit for a more deft touch with legislators, but here again I must guess that lucky timing led to positive relations, as much as a positive approach made its own luck. Hancher, too, set out with high hopes originally. Had Hilton become president in 1940, he might also have doubted by the late 1950s that lawmakers would reliably support growth even when reasons were valid.

As it happened, Hilton frequently met support from lawmakers, Regents, and colleagues instead. President Maucker wanted to develop a broader curriculum at his institution; if

Hilton grudged him some of the details, their shared overall vision made Hancher's concern about "Problems of Growth" a minority among the three schools. Similar programs at colleges in so many other states probably helped persuade the Board of Regents. So long after its initial charter to impose cuts, the board may have needed little persuasion to support the idea of greater holdings anyway. External pressure had sustained its opposition to duplication for a time, but institutions' nature is generally more favorable to growth than to alternatives. One other excerpt from the sketch of Hancher's presidency suggests that deep down, the board was never really an exception:

> Early in his years here, in the course of a drive around campus one day, the President expressed to Henry C. Shull, then president of the Board of Education, the hope that when the new Library was completed, the old armory might be removed to improve the appearance of the central campus.
>
> "Virgil," responded Mr. Shull. "The board of education only builds buildings. We never tear them down."[16]

Hancher, I must suppose, perceived a failure of leadership in this admission. Yet if it was one, it was a failing that he shared at times.

Hancher was entirely willing to trim programs. In a 1945 letter to his dean of liberal arts, he wrote "I am hopeful that the number of courses offered will be reduced rather than increased," and suggested a rule to drop at least one for each new course introduced.[17] Several years later *Time* even celebrated him for "slashing away" at superfluous courses.[18] When it came to departments, however, Hancher was mostly as conservative as Board President Shull. This likely undermined his arguments for reform time and again, above all when it came to engineering and home economics.

Aside from President Hilton's contribution to the "Future Directions" argument in 1959, few people seem to have referred explicitly to the largest duplicative programs at SUI. It may simply have seemed unnecessary, though. I suspect that no one needed to speak of them because their significance was entirely obvious. Even Hilton began his comment: "If we really wish to approach the matter entirely on the basis of duplication..."[19] His language implies a subject everyone is familiar with and has agreed not to bring up—unless pressed to do so. This would have been a constant problem for President Hancher. If he pushed too hard in his complaints of duplication elsewhere, he invited the charge of hypocrisy. In his defense he could have noted that the SUI programs were already established fact, and that dismantling an existing department was not the same as asking that other schools simply leave their own curriculum as it was. Yet on a very real level he was consistently urging *do as I say, not as I do*. This is rarely a popular message.

Something of the same challenge probably supplied one more reason why his ideal alternative fared just as poorly. Hancher's vision of a deeper, more meaningful integration of liberal education within specialist subjects was, in its way, every bit as positive and ambitious as Hilton's more traditional goals for Iowa State. It was much more difficult to picture, though. I spent several months puzzling over how Hancher reconciled support for broad liberal education with opposition to expanded liberal arts majors. If by some good fortune I have explained it well enough for others to understand more quickly, it remains a vague, sketch concept. Responsibility for that lies in part with other administrators' failure to support it—but also with Hancher, himself, who had been president of a university for two decades by 1960. State University of Iowa had professional colleges, and even an engineering program. Yet Hancher never offered any practical example of his ideas nearer than Europe.

He might have answered that this was precisely the reason why SUI programs relied on American models, however clumsy he regarded them. Speaking in Wisconsin, he acknowledged that in America "we lack the extrapolated materials and we lack the teachers competent to do this kind of teaching and convinced that it should be done this way..."[20] Part of his hope, certainly, had been to convince more people of this and recruit their help in developing the teachers and other resources necessary. He had, all the same, been president of a flagship university for most of a generation. I have difficulty blaming people for thinking that, if even this had not provided resources enough, they might just as well get on with using the tools at hand.

Whatever his other shortcomings, President Hancher was not a quitter. He never abandoned his conviction that higher education was pursuing a deeply misguided course. But by 1961, he acknowledged the course had been set, and he was not going to persuade the state of Iowa to turn back any time soon. Hancher was also not, whatever may have seemed the case, unwilling to adapt. He had tried restraining the tendency for institutional aggrandizement that he perceived in Hilton, and Maucker, and even the Board of Regents. He had failed in that. Popular wisdom suggests that if you can't beat them, join them.

Hancher had joined in the trend already, sort of, with requests for expanded duplicating majors in nuclear engineering and vocational home economics. Whether or not he really wanted these, there were certainly other ways in which he desired to expand SUI much more. The problem, he remained convinced, was that proportionately expanded state support was unlikely. He had never fared particularly well with Iowa's legislature anyway, and now with a second university (and, he certainly suspected, a third on the way) a substantially more generous reception from the statehouse seemed less likely than ever.

But the General Assembly based appropriations on requests from the Board of Regents. They invariably cut those requests, it was true. But only rarely was one institution singled out for sterner economies than the others. Otherwise, appropriations were divided more or less in proportion to the Regents' askings. Hancher might never match Hilton's effectiveness at lobbying the legislature, but the Regents were another matter. Those same Regents had been increasingly favorable to requests for more, lately, even when Hancher protested vigorously against them. Here, perhaps, joining the prevailing trend might pay real dividends.

CHAPTER NINE
Educational Load Factor

Until 1960, the subject of appropriations dependably united Hancher, Hilton, their colleagues and the Board of Regents even as they sparred over other issues. All agreed that Iowa provided too little support for higher education, that it had done so for a generation, and that the problem was growing worse.

Their story was consistent. During the Great Depression, the colleges were starved of funds like nearly everyone. The capital improvement budgets of all three state schools, combined, averaged $211,400 per year for more than a decade. During the Second World War capital funds actually fell even further, at the same time that most men and resources were mobilized for war production anyway. Modest increases in capital budgets after the war mostly paid for rapid construction of temporary buildings, to absorb an immediate post-war enrollment boom; most of the results remained in use out of necessity, long beyond their intended lifespan. Well into the

1950s Iowa's government generally provided less than one-fifth of the Regents' capital requests.[1] The consequent deficiencies were tangible reality: overextended "temporary" buildings, shutdowns in winter due to broken heating, libraries approaching 24-hour days simply because they had no other way to accommodate students.

College administrators reported that operating funds and above all faculty salaries were at least as dire. Enrollments steadily increased, and a deluge was anticipated by the mid-1960s. The pool of qualified faculty had not kept up, and as other states appropriated larger salary budgets their colleges took to "raiding" Iowa's.[2] The challenge for administrators is somewhat difficult to appreciate in the 21st century; today, aided by federal loans and grants, a growing student body pays for a substantial portion of its own costs through tuition. Fifty years ago, however, funds for state universities mostly came from state governments. Hancher once responded to calls for higher tuition by opining that "the purpose for which the state universities were established seems to have been forgotten…"[3] To Hancher, Hilton et al., raising the era's relatively low tuitions would be functionally equivalent to turning students away through enrollment limits, and the only other alternative was deeply compromised quality. They regarded none of these as an acceptable outcome.

When it came to legislative askings, a variant of "partisanship stops at the water's edge" prevailed through Hilton's first several years as president. After the disastrous zero-funding of capital improvements in 1957, the three presidents went on radio and television to make their case for increased support.[4] If their coordinated statement was scripted, the cooperation was genuine. Much of the credit for this probably belonged to the Board of Regents. In one of the system's real successes, all three Regents institutions presented their funding requests to the board to sort out, and then deliver to the General Assembly in finished form. Even as overall funding remained short into the 1950s, the Regents system went further in preventing a tussle for scarce resources by reducing budgeting as much as possible to a formula.

The "Toledo formula" took its name from a modest town on Highway 30, where Regents institution administrators patiently bashed out its details. (In Hilton's and Hancher's era, before today's interstate highways, the presidents and their staffs agreed on Toledo as an approximately equal journey for all and regularly sorted out policy at an ordinary café or diner.) The Toledo formula was not, itself, terribly complex. Essentially it was an early version of the same base-plus model that the Regents have continued to employ since. Beginning from each institution's actual budget for a given biennium, the formula applied increases for several fixed categories: enrollment, office and school supplies, transportation costs, etc., as well as hoped-for new programs and buildings.[5] The formula's most notable element was its codification of the institutions' goal for salary increases. The Toledo formula recognized the era's competition as the defining factor in higher education budgeting. It assigned to each Regents institution 1) a specific list of Midwestern peer schools, and 2) salary budgets to move each college into third place on its list.

The rationale for seeking third place was a combination of realism and value. For Iowa's colleges to reach first place in salaries, even within the 11-state region referenced in the formula, would have cost more than twice as much as third.[6] By focusing on third place, the Regents offered legislators the prospect of being competitive, without a bidding war that no one imagined Iowa would win. Although a few lawmakers criticized the idea of settling for runner-up[7], third place was ambitious enough for most, given that it was a constantly moving target. Throughout the latter half of his presidency, Hilton noted over and over that appropriations had met the goal of reaching third place but not the goal of staying there. The 1959 legislature's budget, for example, kept faculty "happy for about 4-5 months" in his telling, but then "the news of the raises the other institutions gave starts to get around when they come to our campus to raid our staff."[8] With some justification, weary lawmakers complained of a zero-sum game without obvious end. For Hilton, who came to regard the loss of quality faculty as the great challenge of his presidency[9], the need had to be met nonetheless. He did his best to improve Iowa State's non-monetary allure for faculty, and heartily endorsed the goal of third place as a reasonable compromise. Beyond that, he made plain that good schools would still require more money for faculty, and just as with physical resources "These were the needs, and the financial resources would have to be found somewhere."[10]

Hilton's counterparts all agreed in general outline. They disagreed on whether this or that specific program constituted a need, or wasteful duplication. But the Regents had the final say on those matters also. Under these circumstances, the Toledo formula seemed to leave little room for arguing over individual operating budgets. The resultant appropriations

EDUCATIONAL LOAD FACTOR

requests appeared as non-controversial as policy ever gets. President Hilton, it's safe to say, took it for granted that this particular peace was in no danger of rupture, no matter how many cracks opened up elsewhere.

The possibility that Hilton ever grew overconfident, or even complacent, is problematic. It seems to impose a tidy moral onto reality that is often more complex, and shaped by chance as much as by any karmic system. Hilton's concerned replies to angry legislators in 1960, for example, challenge any assertion that he was taking things for granted completely. If he was surprised by one or two larger reverses that year and the following, it may owe much to the simple truth that no one can anticipate everything.

Nonetheless, the beginnings of the controversy over "Educational Load Factor" suggest that President Hilton may, at least, have stopped paying close attention to complaints from State University of Iowa. In June 1960, arguing that the university carried a greater "educational load" than its peers, President Hancher staked a claim to substantial extra funding for SUI, alone, above and beyond its Toledo formula allotment. Hilton later characterized the meeting as an ambush,[11] and what eventually became a long, intense campaign of protest all began with Hancher's June presentation. Two years later Iowa State's administration was still fuming that

> the presentation was made to the Board at the June, 1960, meeting without prior opportunity for review by the other in-

stitutions. This was despite the fact that the three institutions had been holding special "Toledo" meetings at frequent intervals over a period of months. Throughout this period Iowa State cannot recall that S.U.I. advised its sister institutions of any plans for requesting an adjustment of its normal base.[12]

Even so, had Hilton been paying close attention he shouldn't really have been surprised. Although the term "Educational Load Factor" was new, Hancher had been making all of the essential points for many months.

Barely two weeks into 1960, President Hancher had asserted that "it takes three times as much money to teach a graduate student as it does to teach an undergraduate."[13] This was the basis of his "ambush" the following June, and the core of arguments that preoccupied the Regents system for years after: that high-cost areas of instruction made up a much larger portion of SUI's offerings than other Regents institutions', and that in consequence the Regents should allow SUI a greater share of its total appropriations requests than it received under the Toledo formula. By late January, Hancher made this implication explicit, too, at a meeting with other Regents administrators. He presented, in person and in writing, a proposal that the board calculate schools' needs based on "that institution's share of the three institutions' total educational effort and responsibility and not by any fixed or inflexible formula," and made clear that he intended this to mean more money for SUI.[14] This seems an open and unambiguous declaration of intent, and one largely complete; for all of the blizzards of memos and analyses and news articles that followed, this remained the core controversy.

EDUCATIONAL LOAD FACTOR

Somehow Hilton seemed not to take any serious notice. It's tempting to imagine that after complaints over "Future Directions," and renaming, and new liberal arts degrees, Hilton was beginning to discount Hancher's protests. Given Hilton's own disappointing record when opposing the trend of Regents policy, he might have expected that this new proposal would fall flat also. If so, he wouldn't have been alone. Minutes of the committee meeting where Hancher outlined the educational load concept suggest that most attendees regarded it as an irrelevant distraction. They listened politely, perhaps coughed awkwardly, then declared that established policy should continue unaltered: "It was generally agreed that we follow the basic principle of the Toledo formula, and that the base be calculated as it was for the last session of the Legislature."[15]

Yet general agreement was not unanimous agreement. At a Regents meeting in April, Hancher repeated his assertion that much higher graduate enrollment placed a heavier "educational burden" on SUI, for which it should be compensated with a proportionately larger share of state funds. His remarks even appeared in newspapers.[16] Perhaps Hilton still believed that this would, ultimately, prove just one more Quixotic campaign; perhaps he believed that Hancher was only arguing about the abstract future, and not planning to challenge the present "generally agreed" adherence to the Toledo formula. This just might explain how Hancher's presentation of the same ideas at an another Regents meeting two months later could constitute, in Hilton's mind, an ambush.

To whatever extent it was, Iowa State's president walked right into it.

HANCHER VS. HILTON

Some fundamental misunderstanding of what administrators had or had not agreed about "educational loads" and budgeting does have plausibility, if only because of how Hilton and Hancher seem to speak past one another constantly. Throughout their arguments the two presidents remained united on major values and concerns. Each spoke consistently, and passionately, about the importance of broader liberal education for scientists and technicians. The Oxford scholar and the state-college dairy expert, both, looked at the forces which science was directing in the atomic age and warned that without deeper appreciation for the workings of human society, the result would be tragedy. Hancher reflected often on the need for education "designed to produce the good man and the citizen," and asked "Can it be a matter of indifference to us whether our product be a Goebbels or an Einstein?"[17] Hilton assuredly believed that it should not. "One of men's greatest needs today is to learn how to live and work together harmoniously and justly in a world which has grown frighteningly small," he proposed, adding that even "The land grant system can no longer see its main research function as a means of discovering ways to increase production."[18]

From the perspective of the tech-worshipping 21st century their shared emphasis on humanities education seems even more notable, even if they disagreed on practical details. Much the same can be said for their general views on funding. Hilton and Hancher both wanted more money for salaries, buildings, etc., yet they adamantly opposed raising it through tuition increases. Naturally enough, they also agreed that all of Iowa's

EDUCATIONAL LOAD FACTOR

public colleges had long been underfunded. In principle they also insisted that each institution deserved more funding, and that extra funding for one should never come at the expense of the others. In principle they never wavered from this, either. Somehow they spent most of four years fighting over their schools' relative shares of funding, nonetheless.

Hancher's remarks in the first half of 1960 perfectly highlight this dichotomy. Calling for more than $1 million in additional funding for SUI in April, he insisted that "this request is by no means a suggestion or intimation that Iowa State or Iowa State Teachers College should not be adequately supported. There is no desire to improve the university's position at the expense of its sister institutions."[19] Yet he also explicitly focused on proportions, as much if not more than on real dollar amounts. Hancher described traditional budgets as assigning SUI and ISU "equal appropriations"—although Iowa State administrators then and since would sharply disagree—and complained specifically that this proportion had unfairly hurt State University of Iowa. To make things absolutely clear he prescribed new ratios: 50% for SUI, 38% for ISU and 12% for Iowa State Teachers College.[20]

In so emphasizing funding portions, of course, Hancher was merely acknowledging the reality of state appropriations. Lawmakers always cut the Board of Regents' requests, usually in proportion. In theory both Hancher and the board might insist that more funds for SUI should not mean reduced funds for ISU and ISTC, and again and again Hancher did precisely that. But the reality would never work that way. Hancher assuredly understood this perfectly well; most of his opposition to a larger and more prestigious institution in Ames was based on the assumption that Iowa higher education funding was a zero-sum game. Now he was trying to claim otherwise, and unlike Hilton he made no attempt to argue that his agenda would cost no additional money. Additional money was the entire point, in this case. To all appearances this placed Hancher in a difficult position, perhaps one further reason that his campaign took Hilton by surprise. President Hilton may not have imagined that Hancher could possibly rationalize what was, despite all protests to the contrary, obviously an attempt to enrich State University of Iowa at the expense of its peers.

Hancher's solution to this dilemma was an inversion of its entire premise: he proposed that it was in fact ISU and ISTC which were already being unfairly enriched at the expense of SUI. "There is an inequity in the distribution of funds between the three state educational institutions,"[21] he informed the Board of Regents in June. Just as remarkably, while Hancher offered a bevy of statistics and study results to support his claim, their common theme was that as a liberal arts university SUI had special expenses that could not be calculated by a formula appropriate to ISTC or Iowa State. Having just spent years warning that those schools were adopting the unique features of SUI, this was a bold change of tactic. But Hancher had lost those battles; his peer presidents had insisted that they were not seeking to usurp any special emphasis of SUI, and their arguments had carried. Now, it seemed, Hancher had agreed to take them at their word and propose that if each of the Regents institutions remained distinctive, their budgets should reflect that.

Up to this point Hilton might have applauded in theory even if he preferred to retain the Toledo formula in practice.

EDUCATIONAL LOAD FACTOR

But Hancher accompanied his lofty concept with specific, hard numbers to argue that fairer, appropriately customized budgets would favor State University of Iowa. As he had been doing all year, Hancher asserted that graduate instruction cost three times as much as undergraduate instruction. Graduate enrollment at SUI (2,644) far exceeded that at both ISU (1,402) and ISTC (250) combined, and therefore the "parity" approach he ascribed to the Toledo formula significantly penalized SUI.[22] This inequity, he added in his June presentation, was further exacerbated by the diversity of subjects at a liberal arts university. "There are more colleges and schools in a University than in a Land-Grant Institution," Hancher offered as further evidence of the Toledo formula's failings. For good measure he noted that "In spite of this, S.U.I. has a smaller faculty than I.S.U."[23] Backing up all of this, Hancher cited a comparative study of Californian and Western Conference schools as well as data from the University of Indiana and its own land-grant counterpart, Purdue.

Again Hancher emphasized for the record that he had no desire to take funding away from ISTC or Iowa State—then proceeded to call for a new funding model that would in practice do precisely that. He now called for $1.96 million of additional funding for SUI. He also spelled out once more his preferred ratios for dividing whatever real appropriations the General Assembly might provide. State University of Iowa's typical share of 45.7% should rise to 50%, with ISU's 40.8% and ISTC's 13.5% each falling slightly to make room.

Documentary accounts preserve little direct evidence of the Regents' immediate reaction. But clues from context suggest that, for once, they were sympathetic to President

Hancher's complaints of unfairness, as well as his petition for redress. The fact that Hancher gave his presentation at all, after what Hilton and others believed was an agreement to table the entire concept, implies that SUI's president had some expectation that the board would give him a favorable hearing. In retrospect, the long subsequent life of the Educational Load Factor suggests that they did so. Hilton's reaction, however, might offer the most conclusive evidence of all. After showing little concern over identical arguments for several months, following Hancher's audience with the Regents in June Hilton suddenly began work on an exhaustive rebuttal.

Shared broad values may have united Hancher and Hilton rhetorically, but they remained very different persons on other levels. In their repeated clashes over practical policy they diverged not only on specific details, but on their entire approach to arguing. Here, to some extent, the scholar and the scientist returned to type.

Hancher emphasized rules and recruited studies to support his case, but seemed drawn most of all to grand theories and long-term challenges. *How can we best design higher education for an entire society*, he asked, *and what will result from our decisions, not tomorrow but a generation from now*. Even presenting an eminently practical, bottom-line argument for more money, he evoked fairness and his deep conviction that a liberal arts university was a specialty itself rather than just the common denominator of higher education.

Hilton, in contrast, appears ever the man of applied science and concrete realities. He was entirely capable of thinking deeply about large-scale problems. But in the context of arguments with President Hancher he consistently placed more emphasis on practical details. *Our institution has this particular challenge right now*, said Hilton, *and here is a specific response which we can implement now without first having to solve larger problems that are beyond our power.* When Hancher or others raised objections, Hilton's rebuttals were often just as technical in approach. He identified the supports of opposing arguments, and set to work methodically demolishing them. This was Hilton's response even to the largely theoretical arguments over Future Directions, or renaming Iowa State. Not only were critics wrong, he asserted, but the assumptions underlying their criticisms were simply incorrect.

In attacking the inherently data-based claims of Educational Load Factor, Hilton's approach naturally remained the same even if he delegated part of the work. The only difference in this case, most likely, was a greater sense of urgency. His 1959 response to Hancher's critical Future Directions memo, though undated, feels like a patient, painstaking individual effort. Little more than a year later, Hancher's new proposal abandoned future generalities for immediate claims on specific resources, and Hilton accelerated his reaction accordingly. He tasked an assistant, Roberta Fritchman, with a draft analysis which she completed barely 10 days later.[24]

Authorship aside, both Fritchman's initial work and the longer siege to which it contributed were entirely in keeping with Hilton's method. Fritchman began by questioning Hancher's theme that "it takes three times as much money to teach a graduate student as it does to teach an undergraduate." Using the California - Western Conference study for support,

State University of Iowa had developed this concept into a ratio of 1:2:3 for costs of teaching underclassmen, upperclassmen and graduate students, respectively. Fritchman argued that the California - Western Conference figures were the result of incomplete data. Its conclusion, she wrote, "reflects salary cost only and does not pro-rate administration, general expenses, physical plant, library, etc." By applying more comprehensive numbers to Indiana and Purdue, she found graduate students' costs were approximately twice that of underclassmen rather than three times, adding that Iowa State's own costs were similar. Anticipating SUI might insist that its own cost ratio was different and, in this case, much more relevant, Fritchman offered a withering response: "probably large numbers of relatively low salaried graduate assistants and part time instructors are used for lower division teaching at S.U.I."[25]

This might have been judged impolitic, at least in its phrasing. But the Hilton administration had committed to an offensive as the best defense, as Fritchman's further proposals demonstrated. Using the concept of educational load, Hancher had argued that SUI's total "weighted enrollment" was 16,077 equivalent undergraduates. Iowa State University also had graduate students, however. Applying an adjusted ratio of 1: 1.2: 1.8 drawn from University of Indiana, Purdue and Iowa State costs, Fritchman calculated a weighted enrollment for ISU of over 18,000. "On this basis S.U.I. is not entitled to any extra allowance," she concluded, "and in fact its proportion of State Appropriations should be cut." Fritchman and Iowa State were just getting started, moreover. She went on to complain that Hancher had also failed to account properly for the ISU Agriculture Experiment Station, and suggested that doing so would show that SUI was even more overfunded relative to Iowa State.

Hilton expanded on this objection repeatedly, in later statements on the Educational Load Factor. Classifying the Experiment Station became one of the lasting sub-controversies of the debate, in fact, and ultimately illustrates why clear answers were elusive even when seemingly precise numbers and facts were at issue: large public universities are complex, messy agglomerations of diverse activities. Hilton insisted that a fair comparison of appropriations among the Regents schools should not count funds for the Experiment Station, as the money was restricted from paying for classroom instruction. On the other hand, he acknowledged that graduate students benefitted from use of its laboratory facilities—but the same was true of university hospitals, which SUI counted separately.[26]

For Hilton, gray areas like this were ultimately an argument against the entire concept of Educational Load Factor in addition to its details. Taking another swipe at the California - Western Conference study, he pointed out that its data set largely excluded programs in agriculture, veterinary medicine and home economics. This, he submitted, made it a highly questionable yardstick for evaluating Iowa State University. More to the point, Hilton argued, the three Regents institutions were too different for any precise accounting: "It is extremely difficult (we think impossible) to work out any uniform estimate of reliable cost figures which will be applicable to all three institutions." Like Fritchman, Hilton asserted that Iowa State could make a case to increase its share of appropriations at the expense of SUI, with just as much validity as the other way around. "But," he noted pointedly, "we are not." Instead, Iowa State asked "only for what we have agreed to in accordance with the so-called Toledo formula."[27]

This, for Hilton, remained the only plausible way to settle the issue of fairness. The base-plus calculations of the Toledo formula were a kludge, undoubtedly. But arguably the same was true of the Board of Regents system itself, as well as its individual institutions. Here again, Hilton advised pragmatism over elegant theory: the Toledo formula, whatever it lacked in sophistication, had already proved itself an adequate response to a real-world problem. In advising that it therefore be left alone, he had in a way exchanged places with President Hancher. Having argued repeatedly that Iowa State required change to meet its responsibilities, and that opposition to this infringed on its rights, Hilton was now the one objecting that his rival should leave well enough alone. For President Hilton, the difference was that in this case Hancher's agenda would harm Iowa State—but of course Hancher denied any such intent, and had by contrast perceived very real harm in many of Hilton's proposals.

Once more, the Board of Regents would have to effect some kind of resolution. Thus far they had frequently been favorable to Hilton, but also to institutional ambition. The Educational Load Factor had scrambled up many of the usual signposts to the board's thinking. If Hilton was unusually anxious about this latest controversy, he had reason to be.

CHAPTER TEN
Miscalculations

The Educational Load Factor challenged many of the Iowa Board of Regents' habits. One of its very oldest reflexes, however, still applied: when in doubt, commission a study. Confronted with President Hancher's call for a bold revision of budgeting policies, and with President Hilton's sharply critical response, the board elected once again to refer matters to a committee.

By itself this was positive news for Hilton. He had argued in this instance against dramatic change, and the board seemed lukewarm at most about initiating any. At its meeting on July 15, 1960, it proposed "studies under the direction of an outside expert to determine the validity of the [State University of Iowa] request based on the educational load factor," with a goal of having results by the 60th General Assembly in 1963.[1] For President Hancher, this should have been by contrast one more disappointment. He was due to retire in four years, and the Regents were proposing to spend almost three studying his request. Yet in a follow-up memo to the board, he actually proposed that they take even more time.

Given the complexity of the issues and the scarcity of experts qualified for the type of study the board proposed, Hancher suggested a two-stage process instead. First, the board should appoint an arbiter to investigate the competing claims "as a Master of Chancery with hearings, followed by a report, opportunity for objections to the report, further hearings, and a final report."[2] Based on this the board would make an interim decision. In the meantime, a more deliberative search might find an appropriate expert in time to guide requests to the following biennial assembly in 1965.

The proposal could almost be sarcastic mockery of the board, and Hancher was certainly capable of depicting a policy as absurd when it tried his patience. In this case, though, it would have indicated an astonishing level of bitterness. Much of his memo seems on the contrary almost chipper. I imagine Hancher rather enjoying himself in recommending the functions of "a Master of Chancery" to the Regents, for example. (The suggestion by itself could have identified the memo as Hancher's even had his name been absent.) Above all there can be no real doubt that Hancher wrote with uncharacteristic cheer, because he was acknowledging the Regents' acceptance of the Educational Load Factor in practice even as it deferred judgment on the theory.

The Toledo formula remained the basis of the board's legislative askings, pending some type of study. But in the meantime, the Regents were adding $500,000 to SUI's portion of their requests for the very next General Assembly in 1961. This was less than any of the figures Hancher had claimed, and lawmakers would inevitably reduce it even further. But it was something real, and immediate. The board, Hancher acknowledged gratefully, was "giving recognition to the principle of appropriations proportionate to the educational cost load."[3] Under the circumstances, the president was tactfully disinclined to rush a more definitive response. So long as the Regents were defaulting to even a partial compensation of SUI for educational load claims, he would encourage them to spend as much time on studies as they liked.

As to what prompted the board's novel compromise of decisiveness and delay, records again provide little clue. For President Hancher, presumably the answer was simply that his claim was valid. Yet he had believed, and continued to believe, the same of many other arguments which left the board unconvinced. As the Regents themselves stopped short of fully endorsing Educational Load Factor, the question of why Hancher received the benefit of the doubt remains.

For what it may be worth, I suspect that an appearance of professional thoroughness and elegant conclusions proved at least as important as the conclusions themselves. Hancher offered the board an ultimately simple and intuitive theory—instruction at advanced levels costs much more than at undergraduate levels—and backed it up with formal published research. By comparison, Hilton was in some sense offering a makeshift, cobbled-together defense of a makeshift, cobbled-together system. The Toledo formula which he favored offered none of the elegance promised by Educational Load Factor. Many of Hilton's objections to Educational Load Factor seem reasonable, even so. Yet their number and variety must have compared poorly with Hancher's tidy reasoning, just as rapidly assembled estimates by Hilton's own administration probably suffered in comparison with the California - Western Conference study.

All of this is of course speculation. It does, though, offer an explanation for Hilton's very evident frustration. Whether or not the Iowa State president should have seen it coming, Hancher's proposal to the Regents had functioned as an ambush in practice. State University of Iowa had not necessarily won the conflict but it had taken ground, and Iowa State's improvised counterattack had failed. Settling the Educational Load Factor debate would now be a matter of years, not months. Hilton would have to dig in for a longer campaign.

In the early 1960s the Hancher-Hilton conflict settled into an uneasy holding pattern. For more than two years, one controversy had steadily followed another. But when the Regents deferred a decision on Educational Load Factor, both it and the larger rivalry between Iowa's universities appeared to become stuck in place.

The most notable exception was in some ways a partial exception, still compatible with the greater pattern. In 1961, Iowa State Teachers College won approval for changing its name to State College of Iowa. Having earlier obtained permission to issue degrees without a requirement for teacher training—pointing out that many of its graduates already took other career paths—President Maucker's request for a corresponding new name encountered relatively muted controversy. Along with other factors in Maucker's favor, though, he may have benefitted from the fact that the Regents system was deadlocked over another issue. Arguments over the Educational Load Factor were getting bogged down into reissued statements of incompatible views, then into meta-controversies over the study meant to resolve them.

A memo from President Hancher in 1960 reinforced the sense of stalemated opponents, fighting and refighting over the same ground. Hancher recirculated his criticisms from the previous year's "Future Directions" debate[4]; Hilton subsequently responded with most of the same points and even phrases he had employed the first time.[5] The ongoing struggle for larger appropriations, meanwhile, had long seemed repetitive anyway, and while the ELF cracked the Regents institutions' former unity, the general pattern persisted. College presidents warned of the growing needs of higher education; lawmakers, after noisy argument, usually increased the Regents' budget; Iowa's colleges briefly caught up in a few areas, then fell behind again as enrollment pressure and competition for faculty kept growing. Amid the overall sense of deadlock, if any shift at all characterized these years it was that they were not easy for James Hilton, or Iowa State University.

By the late 1950s both SUI and ISU had begun organizing alumni outreach to the state legislature, and in November 1960 Iowa State surveyed what its informal lobbyists were hearing in response. The results were not encouraging. Money was, unsurprisingly, the most common of what the report delicately titled "Points of Tension." Some variation of "Where is the money coming from" was a common refrain throughout the state. But a considerable number of complaints also focused

HANCHER VS. HILTON

on policies specific to Iowa State, and to President Hilton's recent leadership. Senator Rigler remained adamantly opposed to any and everything, with his comments summarized as

> Major in English and speech at ISU illegal. Number of courses should be reduced. Liberal arts programs at ISTC should be forgiven. ISU should stop promoting cooperative system of business organization through Extension. Askings beyond possibility of attainment.[6]

But his unhappiness with development under Hilton seemed to be spreading. A number of legislators complained of duplication. One explicitly referenced the perceived "Establishment of liberal arts colleges at Ames and Cedar Falls," and the context suggests that others also had in mind duplication at Iowa State, in particular.

Being a university president inevitably involves ups and downs. Hancher continued to meet with frustrations during the same period, even with the new degree of favor the Board of Regents was displaying. In early 1960 he completed three months as a delegate to the United Nations, but back home his national prestige still counted for little. The following year commercial interests in Iowa City sued the university. Hancher's administration had, through resort to a 30-year loan, finally secured funds to expand the university's Memorial Union, and plans included a 110-room hotel. Local hotels and commerce groups protested that "the new facilities would compete illegally with private business" and took the university to court.[7] In 1962, Hancher faced critics even closer to home when a number of faculty and students complained of his handling

MISCALCULATIONS

of a racially charged controversy. After the Delta Chi fraternity "de-pledged" a black student, the university investigated but declined to release its findings, out of deference to the student's privacy according to Hancher. Dissatisfied students began a petition to reopen the investigation, and Hancher was typically exasperated. State University of Iowa, he insisted, had long championed equal opportunity and was by no means backsliding, yet "because a small but vocal number of faculty and students have been dissatisfied... the fine reputation of the university has been besmirched."[8]

Hancher's relations with lawmakers remained stormy as well. Pleading for greater state support in 1961, he invoked declining American prestige as reason for greater investment in education, in the process outraging two patriotic state legislators. John Rockwell of Harbin County fumed "I am getting damned tired of hearing leaders in various places and levels run down the United States," and hinted that this would not advance Hancher's hopes for greater government funding. William Denman of Adair County went further, warning that "if this keeps up, you may talk me out of $3 million."[9] The episode inevitably made headlines, and while Hancher made his response as diplomatic as he could, he may have sorely envied the presidents of private institutions. Still, for all of their reliable appeal for the press, incidents like these were ultimately minor. A petty tantrum by two legislators would probably blow over. For President Hilton, by contrast, complaints from Iowa lawmakers were growing more consistent, and more numerous.

Hilton's triumph in the Iowa Senate was beginning to look like a high-water mark. The few letters of complaint which immediately followed his next initiative, to win new liberal arts majors, had become several reports of lasting resentment. If the numbers still seemed relatively small, the trend might have implied that worse was to come. Early that winter it did. A document in Hilton's papers hints at a startling reception for Iowa State during that year's appropriations debate: "Then came the hearings before the Governor and the Sub-committee. We were embarrassed and irritated. So were some of our friends and alumni. Down grading Iowa State—upgrading the University."[10]

Regrettably, I have found no additional details of the hearings Hilton references. They may have been December 16, 1960 hearings with governor-elect Norman Erbe,[11] but the Iowa Law Library notes that meetings such as these have never been recorded.[12] Neither university archives nor contemporary press reports include any incidents that match the sole, fragmentary comment. Nonetheless those 30 words speak volumes. Having examined a great deal of Hilton's papers I feel confident that these hearings were nearly unique in his presidency. While many records left an impression of frustration, and at times even anger, only very rarely did Hilton explicitly document such an intensely negative reaction. At all events it seems reasonable to imagine that for Iowa State's president, December 1960 was a second ambush even more brutal than the first.

As was the case the year before, it's reasonable to wonder if Hilton really should have been so surprised; the past year had delivered multiple warnings that lawmakers' discontent with Iowa State was more than just a passing outburst. Once more, the skilled communicator with a reputation for understanding

MISCALCULATIONS

his constituencies had nonetheless been blindsided by their disfavor. Hilton would have been the first to deny he had ever been perfect, of course. Everyone makes missteps, and it's quite possible he had simply met with a run of bad luck. But that too might have been a reason for caution. Colloquially, at least, misfortunes are supposed to come in threes.

For most of James Hilton's presidency, rivalry between Iowa State and State University of Iowa was missing from the very place most people would look for it first, i.e. college athletics. The Iowa Hawkeyes had discontinued contests with Iowa State's Cyclones after 1934. Officially they preferred to schedule more "quality" opponents, which status they did not believe the Cyclones merited. Iowa State fans, for their part, have long maintained that a 31-6 humiliation for Hawkeye football on October 20, 1934, played a role.[13] Whatever the reason, an athletic dimension was mostly absent from the Hancher-Hilton conflict.

The schools could still compete indirectly, in overall performance, but mediocrity in any sort of marquee sport meant this was usually less than a compelling substitute. Even in 1959, one of Cyclone football's best years under Hilton, he was publicly pleading for funds to prevent Iowa State's being ejected from the Big Eight Conference for repeatedly being unable to fund home conference games.[14] Iowa State's winning seasons of 1959 and 1960 did coincide with the last of the Hawkeyes' one, extended period of gridiron prosperity under Hancher, and this may have raised interest in a true match-up. Occasional calls from media and politicians to resume the series briefly rose in volume, perhaps also boosted by the battle over changing Iowa State's name. But SUI remained uninterested, and so things remained—with one exception. In October 1961, Cyclone athletics made headlines by frustrating Hawkeye fandom. Unfortunately for the Hilton administration, if Iowa State inflicted a small defeat on its rival, it inflicted a larger one on itself.

The phenomenon of mass television audiences, which has transformed college football in recent decades, was at this time in its relative infancy. But enthusiasts were already trying to deliver more games to wider areas, to the extent that technology permitted. Iowa was no exception. By 1961 several cities were televising the Hawkeyes' sold-out home games in closed-circuit presentations; fans in Des Moines, for example, could follow the action live at the KRNT Theater. At the same time, however, the National Collegiate Athletics Association had also begun to tighten its grip on college sports broadcasting. Around October 1, the NCAA warned KRNT that it could not show an upcoming match between SUI and the University of Wisconsin. Doing so, the NCAA explained, "would hurt attendance at Iowa State's game against Missouri that day."[15]

Inevitably this explanation left many people unhappy, and most of them were unhappy at Iowa State. KRNT manager Robert Dillon protested that "Denying people the right to see the No. 1 team doesn't mean they will go to see some other team. It is not reasonable to legislate people to go to any show."[16] Dillon also denied that his planned telecast violated any specific rule, and this was one reason Iowa State soon found itself in the cross hairs.

MISCALCULATIONS

The NCAA denied that ISU had filed any objection to this particular telecast. But the only relevant policy it cited, in its press statement, was that "no form of simultaneous telecasts shall be conducted without the express permission of the NCAA Television Committee." No one had obtained such permission, but as Dillon pointed out, KRNT had presented many games in the same way and had others already scheduled. Yet the NCAA's rules had not obliged it to shut any of them down. Therefore, people reasonably concluded that some other factor prompted the ban, and the conflict with Iowa State seemed the most obvious possibility. Especially since ISU officials "had protested vigorously for two years about KRNT's closed circuit telecast of Iowa games,"[17] according to the very same NCAA statement that Iowa State had not protested, this once. To most observers this was less than a persuasive defense.

Meanwhile the Hilton administration's own statements were, if possible, even more of a muddle. On the same day that the *Ames Tribune* printed the already mixed message "ISU denies filing tv protest this season," the *Carroll Daily Times Herald* informed readers: "Cyclones Stand Pat on Theater TV Plan."[18] Iowa State, the *Times Herald* reported, "stuck by its guns in claiming that attendance at the Big Eight game would be curtailed by the [Hawkeye] telecast." Over the next week Hilton took personal charge of Iowa State's responses, but only made things worse. On October 6, he told the *Tribune* that the decision was not Iowa State's to make: "We can't lift the ban."[19] Just three days later, however, the *Times Herald* related that "Hilton Declines to Withdraw Objection," and would be "giving his full support and backing to the Iowa State Athletic

Council, which has opposed such telecasts when Iowa State plays at home."[20]

If some of the confusion represented sloppy journalism, it still seems likely that Hilton and ISU were equally to blame. Certainly the Iowa State president had failed signally to get a consistent message out, whatever obstacles played a part. Even more damning was the reality that there was no good message to send. Iowa State had spent years calling on the NCAA to ban a program that many people enjoyed, and had finally gotten what it asked for; under the circumstances the possibility that it had not specifically repeated the request on this occasion was little reason to argue that resulting anger was unfair.

An open letter from state Senator George O'Malley not only demanded that Hilton retract Iowa State's objections, but also warned that the episode "could well hurt your school."[21] This was admittedly extreme, if par for the course from O'Malley. Another letter, however, was likely a fair summation of both general opinion and the blunder itself. William B. Quarter, executive vice president of a Cedar Rapids broadcaster, advised Iowa State that seeking to gain by blocking a rival program "is indefensible and reveals a pettiness unbecoming of a great university."[22] Just 18 months earlier, offended Iowans had delivered nearly the same message to President Hancher. Now Hilton was in the doghouse.

All in all, the early 1960s was likely the most miserable period of Hilton's presidency. In personal life, both his mother and father died within a short time. National tragedy cast a shadow, as well, when the presence of out-of-town parents obliged Hilton to soldier on through commencement ceremonies the day after President Kennedy's assassination.[23] His work, which had long provided most of the purpose for his life, was suddenly taking a worrying wrong turn. Lawmakers were talking regularly of "Down grading Iowa State—upgrading the University," and the Board of Regents seemed of the same opinion. Earlier in 1961 Hilton had predicted: "Now we come to the decade of the 60's which is sure to be one of the most difficult periods in the history of these institutions—not only for our institutions but for the *state* and the *country*."[24] Though addressing appropriations at the time, the rest of his remarks suggest that he had in mind a broader context. If that wasn't his intent at the time, it likely would have been by year's end. He might also have added, for good measure, *and for the university's president.*

No matter how discouraging his reverses, James Hilton never lost hope. He had long experience in overcoming adversity. If he was living in a metaphorical doghouse as his ninth year in office began, he had once lived in a literal hog barn. In the worst moments of those years he had always found friends, and the same remained true as ISU's president.

Even when he stumbled, nothing I have read suggests that Hilton ever lost the confidence of the Iowa State community, and much suggests the contrary. He had won recognition as a university, majors for dispirited service course faculty, and progress on funding for salaries and other needs, even if it remained tenuous. Hilton himself could observe, the same autumn of 1961 when Iowa State seemed to be on the defensive on so many fronts, that despite it all "in some ways we fared better than in any previous legislative session in our history."[25] Alumni remained enthusiastic about his plans, too, and if they passed on messages of austerity from their senators and representatives they were prepared to help make up for it. The Iowa State Center might have appeared another stalled-out campaign, from the outside, yet behind the scenes Hilton had planted seeds that were ready to sprout. In 1961, he wrote afterward, "we really got down to business in raising money" at last.[26]

Still, the prospect of a theater or arena several years down the road did nothing to address immediate competition for qualified faculty, or to replace crumbling "temporary" buildings that were inadequate for present enrollment, never mind that of five years hence. Hilton had to win back legislators' support, and he had to win back support from the Board of Regents that intermediated between them, as well. Specifically he had to win it back from State University of Iowa, despite the fact that its president and Hilton were ultimately fighting in the same cause. Each president had insisted that he preferred they fight together; each, in some sense, probably blamed the other for having sought instead to advance at his counterpart's expense. The fact remained that for now, that was the reality.

After his early 1961 speech implying a decline in American prestige, the rest of President Hancher's remarks received less notice in the ensuing shouting, yet they were far more insightful about the budgetary challenges facing Iowa's public colleges. Departing further from his warnings of years past, Hancher insisted that Iowa could fund all three Regents institutions adequately after all, even with their expanded programs. Yet it was not doing so, he said, and in describing the consequences he might have been speaking as much for Hilton as for himself. "Our institutions are in a highly competitive situation," he told his audience, yet "We do not make the competition." Instead "It has been forced upon us by the enticements of Government and industry in attracting faculty members," in part, but also by "other institutions of higher learning."[27]

CHAPTER ELEVEN

Irreconcilable Differences

It's natural to wonder, amid the growing number and intensity of their disagreements, about how Presidents Hancher and Hilton regarded one another personally. Multiple published accounts allege that in at least one direction controversy hardened into contempt. I have my own suspicions, although as most of the supporting incidents occur near the end of the rivals' terms in office, I have reserved them to the last chapter as a more natural setting. At this point suspicion and speculation is likely all that I, or anyone else, can offer anyway. If either man did bear the other ill will personally, it's unlikely that he would have committed it to paper and even less likely that any such documentary record would be preserved among his formal archives. Potential firsthand witnesses are nearly all gone after half a century.

For what it's worth, however, one of the few remaining insiders to the rivalry declares himself ignorant of any personal component. James G. Hilton performed graduate studies at

Iowa State in the late 1950s, and had the interesting perspective of living with a parent who was also the school's president. Though he completed his degree before the more fractious, final years of Hancher's and Hilton's presidencies, the junior Dr. Hilton likely would have been in a better position than anyone living to know if his father indeed grew to detest his counterpart. When I posed the question to him, though, he seemed genuinely at a loss to recall anything which would support that interpretation. He did not insist it could not have been the case, but so far as he was aware no personal enmity entered into the conflict. There was simply, but very definitely, "competition."[1] Beyond that Dr. Hilton did not elaborate, but his distinct emphasis on the word seemed to say it all; if there is competition and *competition*, this was very definitely the latter.

Lois Hilton, James G. Hilton, and James H. Hilton.
University Photographs, Box 60, Iowa State University Library Special Collections.

IRRECONCILABLE DIFFERENCES

On this, moreover, the documentary record includes ample evidence. President Hilton himself acknowledged "some real battles between the institutions" over appropriations.[2] By 1962, newspapers picked up on them and left the contemporary public in no doubt that the administrations of SUI and ISU had adopted opposing, irreconcilable goals. Behind the scenes, meanwhile, the memos and minutes reveal different opinions on specific issues becoming general distrust, and plain hostility.

In the first part of 1961, President Hilton's administration updated its draft arguments against the Educational Load Factor. The new version mostly expanded upon the same lines established by Roberta Fritchman the previous summer, with more detailed critique and supporting references. In its language, however, the revised analysis is an entirely different kind of statement. In their initial comments both Fritchman and Hilton were highly critical of the details and basic concept of the ELF, and left impressions of impatience, and even some measure of irritation. The revised critique of early 1961, by contrast, is an expression of complete and undisguised contempt.

The first sentence professes humility about the study's depth, but only in order to mock that of its target in comparison: "This critique of the SUI Educational Load Factor Study is not profound. It is concerned with a quite superficial and rather biased collection of data, which is often misused." The rest of the text continually hammers this assertion that the ELF was junk science. For example:

> Nothing meaningful comes from the calculations made in [section] IV-B-b wherein a weighted enrollment figure for SUI obtained from unsupported ratios is multiplied by a similarly meaningless per student appropriation from ISU. Almost any results can be obtained by such casual combination of unrelated numbers.
>
> Neither comparison contributes enough information to allow any valid conclusions, much less an evaluation of reliable dollar needs.
>
> This section contains an interesting assortment of figures. There is no validity whatsoever in their comparisons.

Iowa State pounced on even the smallest details: "school 'E' in section 3 is not the same school 'E' referred to in sections 1 and 2."[3]

The statement's conclusion went further still. In comparing the ELF proponents' demands with their protests of benign intent, Iowa State pulled no punches: "This new split was made in spite of the statement appearing on the first page of the report: 'SUI's request does not question the internal needs or operations of Iowa State or ISTC nor [desires] its inequity to be corrected by diminishing support to either of them.'" Hilton's administration was, on the record and in no uncertain terms, accusing SUI of not only inaccuracy but hypocrisy.

By this point, however, any analysis by Iowa State alone was to some extent relegated to draft suggestion status, regardless of its frankness or actuarial rigor. The Board of Regents had committed to evaluating Educational Load Factor from some sort of neutral perspective, in theory. The Regents and separate institutions all agreed on consulting an outside expert as their eventual goal. A year later, though, they were no further than an intermediate stage something like President Hancher's suggestion. The "Committee of Nine," with three members from each Regents school, was essentially studying the prospects for a study. Even the snail's pace of this agenda was soon slowed further by bickering and suspicion.

In March 1961, SUI and ISU were already splitting over whether any conclusion was possible before the middle of the decade. Hancher's administration proposed waiting until after the '62-63 fiscal year, then including those figures in a report for the 1965 General Assembly. As the Regents had awarded them the benefit of the doubt in the meantime, this delay appeared likely to benefit SUI, and naturally enough Hilton's administration saw far less necessity for two more years of data. "We believe that some information of value could be provided for the Board of Regents concerning the 1960-61 fiscal year costs," Iowa State's committee members wrote to Hilton, adding pointedly that "It is interesting that the SUI group is not in favor of using this earlier data."[4] Iowa State's report from the Committee of Nine meeting, that March, also records that "SUI members of the Committee were at first not favorably disposed to inviting Wes Arden [an expert on college financial analysis affiliated with the University of Michigan] for one of the meetings."[5] Every suggestion by either school seemed to trigger knee-jerk resistance from the other.

Various proxy conflicts throughout the next year did nothing to help. Though formally assigned to the Committee of Nine, by the following winter the issue of load factors and budget shares was cleaving every forum in which the rival universities met. Formal minutes of the "Toledo Society" are less candid than internal memos, but even formal unity was coming under pressure. Minutes from April 1962 open by recording that "President Hancher had some doubt as to his authority as chairman."[6] Even without details, the implication of petty, passive-aggressive game-playing is strong. Hancher's fellow presidents immediately responded with a motion to affirm his position, which passed easily. But this gesture did nothing to resolve the underlying tension. Afterward, "Considerable discussion was held and a number of frank and rather definite positions were expressed for and against the possibilities. No uniformly acceptable conclusions were reached and the matter will need to be determined later."

Perhaps even more telling, around this time the Society minutes begin to introduce the phrase "*definitely agreed*," in reporting the few instances of consensus. The intensity of the phrase—always emphasized—suggests that the degree of concord had grown so small it needed magnification. By mid-1962 the minutes themselves appear to be under contention. Those from a May 29 discussion of Educational Load Factor include this complicated, self-referential record of dissension:

> Although the item [i.e. the relevant subheading] shows "State University of Iowa only" President Hilton reserved the right to present the educational load factor from the viewpoint of Iowa State University.[7]

Hilton was nearly ready to give up on any coordinated effort, entirely. A month later he sent the Board of Regents

IRRECONCILABLE DIFFERENCES

a letter in advance of what he indicated would be his administration's final statement on the issue. The language, throughout, is that of someone utterly exhausted with a situation but prevented from completely disowning everyone else involved, and therefore trying to disclaim all responsibility for it, instead. Examples include: "I am truly sorry that it has become necessary to send any of these statements to the Board... It is regrettable that we must spend so much of our time drafting documents and rebuttals... It is quite disappointing to us..."[8]

The frustration in President Hilton's letter seems proportionate to the state of the main controversy, by that point. Over the course of 1962, in fact, the entire concept of a main controversy seemed to fracture into completely separate arguments.

Hancher's papers from this period make fascinating reading, particularly a long letter from his director of university relations, James Jordan. The letter sets out a number of concepts that later became formal statements, including many on the fight over using cost study results in 1963 budgeting. Throughout 1962 this argument threatened to overshadow the Educational Load Factor itself. As Jordan makes clear, however, from the SUI point of view the two were unrelated matters anyway, blurred through a combination of accident and opportunism.

In Jordan's summary of events, SUI had always understood the two as separate and had labored to prevent one from creating an unwanted interpretation of the other: "Our timetable was planned to present the educational load factor before urging cost studies in recognition of the fact that without an increase in our level of operation, cost figures on almost any theory would not show cost relationships with ISU and SCI correctly reflecting the higher cost of the educational burdens SUI bears."[9]

In presenting the Educational Load Factor, however, Jordan suggests that SUI "created an emotionally-charged situation with which the Regents can always be expected to be most uneasy." Thereafter, "The Regents were ready to seize upon anything that seemed to give them an answer to the educational load factor arguement [sic], and though it is difficult to know just how it came about, the cost study and the educational load factor began to become associated in the minds of various people, including some of our own." The Hancher administration's intended program began to go further astray when members of the General Assembly took interest in the Regents' planned cost studies. When representatives of the Regents schools accompanied a legislative committee visit to Indiana, Jordan writes,

> I haven't the slightest doubt that the figures revealed to that group and to us at Purdue gave the ISU administration its first ray of hope in combatting our educational load factor via the cost study route. I believe they did rely on Purdue for much of their thinking and probably sought to direct the study with the use of the same techniques which allowed them to change the ratio with respect to Indiana U. over previous studies. This I don't know, but I suspect it. I also suspect that the urgency for 1962 figures was enhanced by the representatives of ISU and SCI who may have anticipated the figures which resulted from our cost study.

IRRECONCILABLE DIFFERENCES

Jordan recommends that SUI aggressively oppose any use of the cost study results in 1963. The university should have mounted resistance even earlier, he advises, and "we have been a party to design of the study, and may have to eat crow on this..."[10] Nonetheless, SUI could not allow embarrassment to undermine what was for it the entire point of the exercise. That being, very simply, correcting the "inequity" among Regents institutions by shifting money to State University of Iowa. A subsequent statement, heavily influenced by Jordan's letter, said plainly: "The 'Educational Load factor' as introduced by S.U.I. means the relative undersupport of S.U.I. in relation to I.S.U. and S.C.I., and thereby the term, by definition, cannot be used by the other two institutions in support of needs which we all have."[11]

The logic, in all of this, is challenging. Hancher's administration argues that SUI had been historically underfunded, presumably relative to the costs of properly meeting its distinct instructional responsibilities. From this reasonable starting premise, SUI's arguments quickly become problematic. Most likely the university was reluctant to confront directly this premise's natural implication, i.e. that it had been unable to meet all of its responsibilities; claiming that it needed more money to do so in future was one thing, but claiming that its budgets had historically been inadequate for good teaching was another. Absent some magical method of making do with less—which the university would then have to prove was about to stop working—this would mean SUI had already permitted the mediocrity which Hancher constantly decried.

By its very nature, the Educational Load Factor allowed no clear escape from this dilemma. Claiming a fundamental, in-

175

trinsic extra cost at SUI was essential for it to work, given that any claim based on future cost burdens would have sounded no different from the same pleas that all of the Regents institutions made, year after year. Eventually the Hancher administration tried to fudge this issue with talk of "financial anemia," which was perhaps a euphemism for "mediocrity for which we are not responsible." The phrase was so vague, though, that it did little to indicate SUI's calls for aid as more dire than others'. State University of Iowa was simply in an awkward position.

That position, as Jordan observed, had become even more awkward once the Regents and others latched on to a cost study as a means to determine the schools' true needs. Without specifically accounting for the Educational Load Factor, which SUI had hoped to establish first, any study of historic costs would be unlikely to demonstrate greater shortfall in its funding than either of its peers'. Yet the perception of ELF as something still unproved had, contrary to plan, become recognized as the entire reason for conducting the studies. In response SUI took to repeating three assertions, almost as a mantra. As set out in Jordan's letter: "There is no relation between the cost study and the educational load factor... Educational load factor concerns what should be... The cost study indicates what has been."[12]

No matter how often it was repeated, though, this still left Educational Load Factor vulnerable to being lumped in with everyone else's claims for more funds. Iowa State and SCI had their own proposals for "what should be," after all. For this issue, Hancher's administration had two main responses. The first was simple, blunt insistence on Educational Load Fac-

IRRECONCILABLE DIFFERENCES

tor as the preserve of SUI alone. In one question-and-answer document, SUI charged that detractors were just jealous: "We have made no reference to your needs other than to urge that you be adequately supported. If you have institutional needs we suggest you present them factually, not on a 'Me Too' basis."[13] Though a biting rebuff—worthy of Hancher whether or not it was his own coinage—this did not actually explain why costs of graduate instruction should fall uniquely upon SUI. Nor did the arbitrary claim that "by definition" ELF excluded other schools. As Jordan's letter admitted, the university had walked into a problem with no easy solution, and had no immediate alternative but the second potential response. It had to keep the cost studies out of 1963 budgeting, and stall for time.

For all that its larger arguments were growing tangled, in the 1962 battle over cost studies, State University of Iowa had a relatively simple rebuttal. Here they could point out that none of the schools considered the cost data genuinely complete.

An entire binder in Hancher's papers is filled with back and forth arguments over whether the Regents had an obligation to publish the cost study results to date. Hancher's, Hilton's and occasionally Maucker's administrations quarreled over what the presidents had agreed, what the Regents expected, what the public was owed, what the legislature had called for or might demand, etc. SUI statements complained that the study thus far had been biased, protesting among other things a six-to-three committee vote over how academic calendars should be weighted. Hancher's administration also insisted that it was the one recommending the old Toledo formula be left alone for the time being, and that by pushing for adjustments based on the cost study, Hilton and Maucker were in fact the advocates for disruptive change. Naturally, this charge took for granted that Educational Load Factor adjustments were a separate issue. But, in the end, Hancher had one objection that was impossible to deflect as sophistry or special pleading: *"Either the cost figures are the true and correct costs of adding students to existing enrollments or they are not."*[14]

Try as his opponents might to argue out of it, here Hancher had them. Iowa State and SCI only wanted to present the results to date with substantial adjustments, to account for what they admitted were incomplete data. Ultimately any study requires interpretation, but both the ISU and SCI proposals seemed to go substantially beyond that. State University of Iowa insisted that each amounted to arbitrary transformations that ran contrary to the whole purpose of a detailed cost study.

Iowa State and SCI argued back over details. But Maucker eventually tried to minimize the importance of using the study data in 1962[15], while Hilton's emphasis that legislators and others expected *something* effectively ceded Hancher's point that the quality of the results was, in all honesty, not a very good argument.

In his last push, Hilton wrote to the Regents that the available results were not perfect, and certainly weren't uncontested, "but we are firmly convinced that they are as accurate and reliable as any cost figures yet published." It seems probable that he had given up serious hope for the time being, though, and was merely writing for the record in some sense. Once more, he insisted that Iowa State was not the aggressor: "I wish to make it perfectly clear that Iowa State has not and will not argue against larger appropriations for any of our educational institutions provided such additional appropriations are made on an equitable basis and are not secured at the expense of additional funds desperately needed at the other institutions." His follow-up report to the board continued the same theme. "Having to devote so much time on this... has been very depressing for us. I am truly sorry that it has been necessary to burden you with all of these reports. Apparently there was no other way."[16]

By any objective measure, Hilton had reason to be disappointed. Two years had gone by and compromise among the Regents system seemed to be further away than when the board first heard Hancher's presentation on ELF in June 1960. Under Iowa's biennial legislative schedule, the Regents would have to revisit the issue of how to divide up their proposed budget soon, whether or not committee debates had reached any kind of unified conclusion. In fact the approaching deadline provided a strong incentive for Hancher, Hilton, et al. to press their individual, incompatible claims all the harder. The Regents had considered a dispute among their subordinates and said *work this out*, and the subordinates had agreed on precisely one thing: *we can't, you settle it*.

The second time that the Board of Regents considered the Educational Load Factor, no one could claim to be taken unawares. In the summer of 1962 Iowa's media embraced the controversy; the fight over cost studies went mostly undetected, but journalists knew that some kind of battle was in progress.

HANCHER VS. HILTON

On July 18 the *Mason City Globe-Gazette* declared that "The 'educational load factor,' at the State University of Iowa is one of the most controversial issues to ever hit the Iowa Board of Regents."[17] The *Carroll Daily Times Herald* raised the volume the following day with the headline: "ISU and SUI Battle Over State Fund."[18] Hilton's administration, the *Times Herald* detailed at length, took "sharp exception" to State University of Iowa's continued claim to special funds.

Iowa State was not alone, either. While President Maucker had recently attempted to lower the temperature of the debate, not everyone at State College of Iowa shared his instinct for conciliation. In a searing story the *Times Herald* related that SCI representatives "describe educational load factor 'as a novel term not found in standard budget terminology' and one which has been defined by SUI to apply to them exclusively."[19]

The story's unnamed source belittled SUI's proposal as "based on the assumption that it is such a great loss to the state of Iowa if S.U.I. does not maintain the same numerical ranking that it had in 1925 that the state should give top priority to achieving that ranking again." Hancher's administration had, by this point, attempted to substantiate its references to "financial anemia" and "program dilution" by comparing SUI's place in recent university rankings with an older study that had placed several of its departments much higher.[20] This ignored the stark reality of other regions' faster growth in the decades since, as SCI pointed out. It also ignored questions about the value of such rankings, which were already familiar in 1962 and even in 1925. Digging into the archives, the *Times Herald*'s interviewee unearthed a remark by the 1925 study's author, Raymond Hughes: "it's not my thought that this rating is exactly correct or of very great significance." This ought to have been some small embarrassment to the Hancher administration.

It may simply have been too late to matter. The *Times Herald* actually printed its interview a day after newspapers reported the Regents' decision. It seems more likely that the board itself heard SCI's protests and those of ISU, and responded with a noncommittal shrug that declared individual details beside the point. On July 24, *The Guthrian* reported that "After debating the question for months, in secret sessions, the board of regents has decided that an extra $300,000 a year be included in the S.U.I. appropriation requests."[21] Cost study results were deemed premature; instead, the old Toledo formula persisted, plus an extra share for State University of Iowa. The Regents once more awarded Hancher and SUI less extra funding than requested, but enough to declare that Educational Load Factor was de facto policy until a more settled committee report could absolve the board of making a final decision on its own.

Against this, Hilton and Maucker probably could have presented the most complete, detailed arguments they liked without it making any difference. In 1960 the Regents had taken a position squarely on the fence. At the time they happened to be facing SUI's way, but neither that detail nor the reasons seemed to matter after two years. Without someone else to enforce peace between the opposite sides, the Regents simply weren't going to move at all.

It was, nearly, back to square one. Despite argument over the results, the Regents institutions had expended "18 months of careful studies by able people and an expenditure of considerable sums of money,"[22] in Hilton's phrasing. They had pushed the era's computing power to its utmost limits; Iowa State had suggested aiding SCI, which might otherwise have been processing reams of data by hand, and representatives of SUI claimed at one point that the necessary machine hours were so considerable they would require special approval from President Hancher.[23] Yet the Regents had refused to consider any of this before the input of a yet-to-be-selected independent reviewer, or some other "final" above-reproach outcome. This was all the more frustrating for Hilton and Maucker, as State University of Iowa seemed openly unconcerned with supporting the pursuit of that outcome.

Looking back after retirement, Hilton wrote that even "during the years of conflicts—the staffs of the two institutions, with few exceptions, worked together very cooperatively. Some of them would say to the Regents occasionally that if we could keep the administrators away from their meetings there would be no problems between the two universities. There was probably much truth in this statement."[24] The Committee of Nine proved one of the exceptions, however.

A couple of months after voicing suspicion of SUI's sincerity in March 1961, Iowa State's committee liaison Wayne Moore filed a positive report that meshes well with the president's later reminiscence. Gradually, though, his reports to Hilton became consistently pessimistic. By early August, Moore acknowledged that "Some fundamental differences have not yet been resolved in the committee," the most important question being: "Is the analysis of the 1960-1961 academic year costs to be (a) *the determination of the cost of the educational activity* at each institution, or is it to be (b) *an accounting of that portion of the general funds spent on educational activity* at each institution." According to Moore, "Most members of the committee feel that (a) above is the most accurate statement of the purpose of the analysis, while Mr. Lewis is devoting most of his efforts to doing (b) at SUI."[25]

A year later, Moore suggested that SUI had all but dismissed the committee effort completely. In his telling, "if the Committee of Nine does not use the same procedures as in the SUI outline, SUI will continue to do a cost study along its own lines," having begun a parallel project on its own already. Perturbed at this, other committee members had pressed one of SUI's representatives, John Uthoff. "Upon questioning Mr. Uthoff upon what his idea was of the function of the Committee of Nine," Moore noted, "he said he was unable to ascertain any useful function."[26]

In fairness, these are accounts of Iowa State, and its perspective and State University of Iowa's had long since diverged on these issues. Yet James Jordan's correspondence with President Hancher and other SUI documents show a similar distrust. What's more, SUI's alleged indifference to peers' views might be regarded as more than plausible, given the example set by the Regents. In practice, they had proved firmly sympathetic to the Hancher administration and indifferent to its critics for more than two years. Hancher and his colleagues—convinced that they were correct anyway—arguably had little reason to take a different attitude.

State College of Iowa's release of bitter, anonymous complaints provides further reason to believe that SUI was indeed isolated among the three schools. In combination, this two-to-one split may have offered one small consolation for President Hilton as 1962 ended. Otherwise his assessment was probably shifting, from depressing to disgusting.

All of his administration's efforts plus those of SCI had failed where it counted. The Regents had twice blessed Educational Load Factor adjustments, and if the rivalry in which this took place is too complex to reduce to a simple "score," Hancher had been earning most of the points lately, all the same. In the meantime Hilton could no longer find consolation in the larger, objective budgetary picture either. In 1962 Iowa State had turned away students for want of anywhere to put them, cutting off enrollment for men in February and women in May.[27] The disparity between applications to Iowa's colleges and their resources at last produced the very result Hilton had most dreaded.

Prospects for more help from the legislature can't have been advanced by those colleges fighting among one another. At a meeting in October, Hilton voiced his frustration with the deadlock over Educational Load Factor. "There was considerable discussion of the procedure to be followed in resolving this issue," President Hancher recorded in the meeting minutes, and "President Hilton would like 'to forget the whole thing: and join forces to move forward.'" Maucker, with accuracy if probably little enthusiasm, then "observed that this would involve having SUI waive the point."[28]

That, obviously, was not in the cards. After his own disappointing years on the defensive, Hancher was effectively setting the agenda. With 20 months left before his retirement he had little incentive to cede it willingly. At the risk of dramatizing events, it seems fair to suggest that President Hancher's attitude toward joining forces remained exactly what it had always been: a fine idea, so long as State University of Iowa would lead.

CHAPTER TWELVE
Showdown

If the Hancher vs. Hilton conflict had a subdued, repetitive character in 1961, in 1963 it had almost no character whatsoever. The newspapers had little to report. The most notable story within Iowa higher education only emphasized the depth of the stalemate. Early that year, the Board of Regents examined proposals to establish a four-year college in western Iowa, or else a branch campus of an existing institution. This quickly proved another non-event, though, as it merely united the board, Hancher and Hilton again, just long enough to smother the idea with reluctance.[1]

The Regents system presidents had a perfectly good argument already, and no need for any new controversies. Later in the year, Hancher took offense to an Iowa State press release bragging about its summer enrollment, and wrote Hilton and Maucker calling for a uniform measure of summer student numbers.[2] Neither man even bothered replying.[3] Meanwhile, the machinery of cost analysis continued working behind the scenes, but even this was remarkably quiet. The sparring of the previous year is largely absent from minutes and memos. Possibly the board's choice to disregard more than a year's worth of study reduced participants' sense of any advantage to be gained. One way or another an entire year vanished, and Virgil Hancher was soon entering the last six months of his presidency. The events of those six months, however, more than made up for the inactivity that preceded them.

For all that Hancher's many attempts to dictate policy to Iowa State University may appear acts of aggression, especially from that university's perspective, he could nearly always claim to be acting defensively in response to someone else's prodding. The board assigned Iowa's colleges to discuss future directions for development, so he offered his honest views. President Hilton's requests for formal university status and expanded curriculum were, from Hancher's perspective, threats to State University of Iowa's position, so he acted in its defense. Even Hancher's brief, private protest against Iowa State's candidacy for the Association of American Universities was prompted by someone else arguing that Hancher ought to speak out in favor of the idea. The Educational Load Factor stretched this concept, considerably. But in the larger picture Hancher could claim that this, too, was merely fighting back against rivals' nibbling away at SUI, even if those rivals believed it was no such thing.

The claim of self-defense is, above all, perhaps most applicable to what otherwise appears Hancher's most audacious assault. On January 29, 1964, Hancher proposed that Iowa should award SUI an equal share of Iowa State's historic status as a land-grant institution, then assign SUI control of the ISU extension service as well. For good measure he repeated his advice that a single University of Iowa system should replace both universities and State College of Iowa. In combination this was an astonishing suggestion, even after five years of clashes over the shape of Iowa's colleges. Yet the very same wire story that spurred loud and rapid responses throughout the state also acknowledged another, much more specific context for Hancher's proposal.

Over the preceding two weeks, Governor Harold Hughes had floated views on extension services that were very similar but for one twist.[4] Like Hancher, Hughes anticipated that Iowa State's existing programs might lose relevance to an urbanizing population, and that shifting its extension away from an agricultural emphasis might lead to duplication of SUI offerings. As a United Press article noted, however, the governor "indicated the extension service at Iowa State might eventually be given control of extension programs at all three state institutions." Its author then speculated that "Hancher's speech apparently was a bid to give the University of Iowa [*sic*] that job."[5] Hancher himself didn't put it in quite those terms. No doubt it seemed more decorous and more compelling to emphasize the larger picture than to make his case within the context of a turf war, even if someone else had provoked it. Beyond that, assigning blame entirely to the governor would not only have been impolitic, but less than completely honest. The full truth was that, as with other arguments in which Hancher responded in one sense to an external provocation, he had also been prodding at the issue himself for some time.

HANCHER VS. HILTON

By 1964 some form of conflict between the Hancher administration and ISU Extension had been brewing for years. In late 1961, the *Jefferson Herald* had heaped praise on Iowa State's programs, as a prelude to calling for greater outreach by SUI in its own areas of specialty. The *Ames Tribune* then highlighted the *Herald* comments in a faintly smug editorial, smirking that "It would appear the ISU extension staff has set a pretty high mark, and whetted the appetite of some Iowans for better things."[6] Hilton's office clipped out and saved the *Tribune* story, likely appreciating it particularly after the recent telecast fiasco and other difficulties that year. Hancher, by contrast, responded tetchily to the *Herald* story and argued that SUI was in fact over-achieving on smaller resources: "A great many people are inclined to criticize us as being indifferent to the interests and welfare of the people of the State. This is not true at all. Indeed a great many of our people go to considerable length to provide service which ought normally to be provided through a well subsidized and supported Extension Service."[7] Newspapers' unasked critique was certainly irritating if nowhere near the threat implied by Hughes's later comments. Yet even the *Herald*'s prodding doesn't offer a clear start to the 1960s arguments over extension services, because State University of Iowa was already laying groundwork for them over a year earlier.

In March 1960, an SUI committee took it upon itself to survey the state of all Iowa's extension services. As its report noted, "the Committee has not consulted with representatives of either Iowa State University or Iowa State Teachers College" and its judgments were entirely "unilateral."[8] Despite this, and the fact that President Hancher himself was not party to the project, the committee's perspective on rival institutions was every bit as skeptical as any of Hancher's own critiques. In three parallel extension services, it saw competition, duplication and waste: "Extension programs, because they do provide direct contact with the people of the state, are attractive places for institutional drum-beating and empire building." Extension offerings already included "a depressing amount of obsequious trivia," in the committee's estimate. Like Hancher, its members had no sympathy for this perceived sprawl: "The fact that an identifiable group of people want a particular service is not enough, in the Committee's opinion, to justify a university's hastening to provide it…" Also taking a cue from Hancher, the committee proposed a sweeping reform as the ideal outcome—including the break-up of extension divisions into "smaller, more rationally organized sections"—or, given the political influence of tradition, at the very least a single director for all three services.

Presumably Hancher found all of this eminently sensible. One month after his rebuttal to the *Jefferson Herald*, SUI's Dean of Extension R.J. Blakely presented these ideas to the Board of Regents, and if the timing was coincidence Blakely still must have had his president's approval. Unsurprisingly neither Iowa State's nor State College of Iowa's president felt much enthusiasm. Maucker argued for independence lest "the soul of volunteerism be lost in the machinery of bureaucracy," while Hilton speculated on "a situation in which no one could turn around without copies in quintuplicate."[9] If their language verged on grandstanding, their objections had at least part of their desired result, in this case. As with Educational Load Factor, the Regents deemed SUI's points valid, but issued no more than a watered-down response in practice. The board first delayed a decision, then assigned all three schools to address the issue in a cooperative committee.

For Hancher this left the real problem unreformed. In his mind, the Regents system itself remained the core problem, in fact; at both levels there was simply inadequate central authority to curtail duplication and waste. What may have been the key criticism amid his remarks on extension reform in January 1964 effectively summarized years of comment on higher education as a whole: "Coordination is otherwise purely voluntary, and is completely dependent on good faith and good will. When it doesn't work, and often it doesn't, it is because success presupposed a condition in which the institutions bury or blend their ambitions and work together for the common good."[10]

Perhaps for that reason Hancher chose to combine his remarks on extension with another call for a university system, though he offered a different, topical justification. The "postal mix-ups" following Iowa State's 1959 name change had been another footnote in recent years, and Hancher pointed to this in renewing his proposal for a university system. "In view of the confusion that now exists with respect to the names of the three institutions," he suggested, "this proposal is even more in order than it was when first presented."[11]

Despite his administration's long interest in some type of extension service consolidation, I still believe that Hancher's proposed takeover of Iowa State Extension owed much to Governor Hughes's suggestion of the reverse. If Hancher's proposal was still an aggressive move, it was probably launched as a pre-emptive defense as much as anything. Given all of the times SUI had found itself reacting to events too late during the past several years, as well as the general climate of antagonism, I submit that Hancher had reason to try getting ahead of an issue for once. It's also worth questioning how seriously he really expected his ideas to be received. I cannot imagine that he would have made such a suggestion idly, just as a rhetorical tactic. His provost Harvey Davis might have, perhaps, but Hancher took policy debates far too seriously to advocate for a reform this major without really believing in it. Believing in its chances of implementation, however, may have been another matter. In that sense, his decision to speak up in spite of demonstrated resistance to similar proposals may confirm that his practical intent was to defend SUI more than to attack ISU.

President Hilton felt less sympathy. By 1964, he had reason to feel that his institution, too, had been on the defensive for a number of years. His patience with that position had already grown thin, and upon this latest affront from Iowa City it finally ran out. Drafting his reaction within hours of Hancher's speech, Hilton began with as measured and neutral a tone as he could manage. Declaring his regret at having to disagree with his colleague, Hilton noted that he had personally worked within a university system in North Carolina. Based on this practical, first-hand experience, he warned that Iowa might gain nothing but more bureaucracy. In contrast, he offered positive comments for the Board of Regents structure: "our three state institutions have grown, developed, and achieved high national prestige and position under our present system."[12]

Having established himself as reasoned and loyal, however, Iowa State's president at last gave vent to indignation. "I am amazed at President Hancher's suggestion that the State University at Iowa City be designated as the Land-Grant institution," he declared, for the simple reason that it seemed absurd: "...after a century of service and experience in handling Land-Grant programs, to give the program to another university without experience in these fields certainly does not make sense."[13]

Even to this point, Hilton was within familiar boundaries. As far back as the first skirmish over Future Directions in the opening weeks of 1959, Hilton had politely but firmly declared Hancher fundamentally misguided. He then devoted the rest of that response to setting his counterpart straight. For the most part Hilton had emphasized the same approach since, and even amid the bitterness of the Educational Load Factor debate he had only sharpened his criticisms or, finally, declared that he had made his case and saw no point to further discussion. Now it seemed that this was no longer adequate to the challenge at hand. Hilton closed with a blunt warning that Iowa State University was through being treated as a junior partner subject to plans made in Iowa City, and that SUI would have ISU as an equal partner, or not at all: "I am afraid that proposals such as those made by President Hancher will undo the cooperation which now exists among the three state institutions, and will make the development of further productive cooperation even more difficult to achieve."[14]

That, in a significant sense, was that. A few people tried to keep the issue of one university system for Iowa alive, over the months that followed. The Board of Regents replied with a noncommittal willingness to discuss the concept. Newspapers kicked it around a bit, and a doctor from Pella, Iowa, wrote the director of North Carolina State hoping he might rebut Hilton's views.[15] Chancellor John Caldwell replied diplomatically that every state's needs were different, but added that he doubted Iowa would gain much by instituting a university system, and might be worse off. Advising his correspondent that "I am inclined to think that you might listen very carefully to President Hilton's views on this matter," he circulated a copy of his letter to Hilton himself, making clear that Hancher's proposal would receive little help from the Tar Heel state.[16] A few months later, State University of Iowa's alumni magazine reprinted Hancher's remarks from January. But the context of a farewell issue, in tribute to the outgoing president, essentially acknowledged that this was now an orphan opinion.[17]

For practical purposes, the original concept of giving one school control of three extension services had already been abandoned by its "parent" back in January. The very day after Hancher offered his own version of the proposal, Governor Hughes convened a hasty attempt at damage control. He indicated that even before Hancher spoke, he had received "a number of letters," and without specifying their content it seemed that Hughes regretted what he had unleashed, reassuring all that "the Board of Regents will be able to solve this problem without the help of legislation or a citizen's committee." His entire statement was something a mishmash. Hughes tried to defend the principle of more united administration of Iowa's public colleges, as an appropriate response to the old foe duplication. Nonetheless, by not only emphasizing it as a matter for the Board of Regents but repeatedly referencing "a study" of the issue, he was effectively distancing himself from any real challenge to the status quo.[18]

The governor's primary hope seemed to be drawing back and letting things blow over—which outcome, he implied, was potentially close at hand if everyone just had a bit more patience. "Iowa is fortunate to have two good men like such as [sic] Presidents Hilton and Hancher," Hughes offered, "and it's unfortunate that a clash should arise at this time, since both men are close to retirement."[19]

Unfortunate it may have been. Yet in commenting on Hancher's pending exit, Governor Hughes may have identified a second reason for the SUI president's combative role in that unfortunate clash. Hughes's own blundering was probably still the biggest reason Hancher made such a dramatic suggestion when he did. I have the feeling, however, that approaching retirement was also a contributor far more than a deterrent. In 1964, Virgil Hancher was near the end of his presidency and had little to lose; his reason to hold back was fast fading.

Just weeks after the blow-up over extension services, Hancher and Hilton were petitioning the Board of Regents in complete accord, at least between themselves. Even more remarkably it was primarily money that brought them together. The standoff over Educational Load Factor remained unresolved. Throughout it, though, both administrations had formally agreed that all of the Regents institutions were underfunded, and that ideally everyone's budget needed to be increased. They also concurred that state appropriations were unlikely to match that ideal in the foreseeable future, and the tug-of-war over formulae and portions had been one result. Another, however, was a turn toward other sources of funds, and here competition was not only regrettable in theory but largely inapplicable in practice.

In seeking a cultural center for Iowa State, Hilton had looked to substantially increased alumni donations from the very outset. (Graduates who lament the ISU Foundation's unfailing efforts to track them down, seemingly anywhere on Earth, can thank the Hilton administration.) Vocal exceptions aside, overlap between the universities' alumni was negligible and thus offered little reason for the institutions to fight. Meanwhile, the possibility of increased tuition and fees offered every reason to work together.

For most of Hancher's and Hilton's presidencies, shifting more costs of higher education onto students had united the two men in reluctance. Though one had enjoyed both family resources and scholarship money, and the other had nearly been deterred from study by its cost multiple times, they shared their era's prevalent belief that public college should be publicly funded. As recently as 1962, Hilton had considered an increase in student fees to support the Iowa State Center but then withdrawn it as premature.[20] The following year, his administration published a Q&A about budgetary needs, and included resounding praise of low tuition as a pillar of American democracy.[21] By 1964, though, Hancher and Hilton could see that their era was passing in more ways than one. Even with recent years' growth in appropriations, the possibility that they would ever fully catch up to baby boom enrollment numbers seemed hopeless. Meanwhile both men were personally near to departing university administration. Hilton was following Hancher into retirement by just a year, and their opportunity to cement long-desired legacies was nearly over.

In February, therefore, the pair set aside multiple reservations and called on the Regents to approve higher tuition and fees. Both argued that without the increase they could afford neither core costs of instruction, nor new amenities. Hancher recalled "the University's long-felt need for a 'bona-fide built-for-that-purpose, comfortable, acoustically-pleasing auditorium.'"[22] Basic classroom expenses had perpetually taken priority, and still required additional investment as well; to make progress on both goals, the universities had no alternative but to demand a greater share in that investment by students. Hilton was in full agreement. Echoing similar comments by Hancher, he declared that "I'm always reluctant to see fees increased because I know what this means to our many students who are attending Iowa State on modest budgets. However, there is no other way if we are to give them the kind of educational opportunities which they expect when they enroll here."[23]

The Board of Regents was nonetheless unmoved. Having repeatedly addressed conflict between the presidents by deferring a decision, and urging the two administrations to sort out a common agenda, they now responded to one by voting for delay and study anyway. At least one Regent cited concern for needy students, in hesitating. The majority, however, diluted such noble sentiment with additional and somewhat contradictory complaints that Hancher had publicized the proposal before approaching the board, yet given too little advance notice.

There can be little doubt that both presidents were appalled, and with reason. Hancher, though, voiced his reaction publicly—and in front of attending members of the press. Some chose to soften the episode, the *Kossuth County Advance*, e.g., reporting only a "temper display" in which "Hancher walked out of the meeting with some unkind comments."[24] But the *Mason City Globe-Gazette* spared no detail. The president of State University of Iowa, it informed readers, declared that "This is the worst Board of Regents meeting I have seen in 25 years. This thing is dead. This board is waiting for returns from the country."[25] A dozen years before, when a colleague extended a mostly humorous offer to make sure he didn't say anything he shouldn't, Hancher replied in the same spirit that "Probably I'd say it anyway!"[26] Now, out of patience and low on reason to care, he *was* saying it.

It's unrealistic to suggest that one display of temper ended what had been a fairly good streak for Hancher. He had, after all, offended powerful people before. The Regents, who were themselves divided 5-4 on the vote he so roundly condemned, seemed not to hold it against him when the time came for a formal send-off a few months later. For that matter President Hilton had practically threatened sabotage in response to Hancher's proposal for extension, which the board itself judged fit for discussion. In this light, the possibility that Hancher's outburst caused the Regents to turn on him doesn't stand scrutiny. Nonetheless the board's frustration of planned fee increases, which Hancher attacked and Hilton received relatively quietly, does mark the beginning of a last reversal in their fortunes with that body. If a diverging approach to the board did not cause that reversal, it probably did help to perpetuate it.

In the final weeks of his presidency, President Hancher seemed more settled than ever upon a go-for-broke finish. Rather than lowering his expectations of the Regents he raised them, at least overtly. In June 1964 Hancher submitted to the board a request for $6 million for "strengthening programs," above and beyond requests for even larger increases in other categories. His request, to say the least, took the recipients by surprise. Though the Regents and schools all recognized strengthening programs as an established expense category, the amount Hancher proposed diverged from custom by an order of magnitude. At the same meeting Iowa State sought just $800,000 for the same purpose, by comparison.

Hilton, perhaps after passing through disbelief, characterized the SUI request as excessive. Hancher denied it, and here might have begun one final round for the veteran pugilists. This last contest, though, was nearly over before it started. After a closed-door meeting the board not only cut Hancher's request to $4.7 million, but more notably "left the way open for Hilton to revise his figure upward" according to news reports.[27] The Regents were as ever a deliberative institution, and neither figure was final. Nonetheless, trimming back a contested request from Hancher was one thing—the board had addressed numerous budget battles this way—but essentially directing Hilton to raise his own request was another.

SHOWDOWN

Taken together this was nearly as firm a ruling, for one side over the other, as any in all Hancher and Hilton's years of dispute. Only one may have surpassed it, as a defeat for Hancher in budgetary matters. While not a decision of the Regents themselves, per se, for that very reason it may have been the most stinging rebuke of all. Two months before the board heard specific budget requests from Iowa's public colleges, it had received a finished report on a related but more general question. After years of study and argument and delay, representatives of all three schools had arrived at a single conclusion on the Educational Load Factor, and it was not favorable to Hancher or SUI. Just the opposite, in fact. As the *Globe-Gazette* announced on April 11, 1964, "The State Board of Regents has been told it costs more to educate students at Iowa State than it does at the University of Iowa [*sic*] or State College of Iowa."[28]

The story made no mention of an independent expert, apparently found largely or entirely unnecessary. With or without such an expert's endorsement, this was effectively the neutral result the Regents had awaited. State University of Iowa had equal representation on the committee, as did State College of Iowa, yet the report's conclusion was solidly favorable to just one-third of the committee membership. What's more, in a further hint that the members had indeed merely gone where the data led them, they did not overturn the principle of Educational Load Factor. On the contrary, they confirmed a significant increase in costs per student from underclassman, to upperclassman, to graduate student. But that cost actually fell heaviest on Iowa State University. Along with its core numerical results, the committee noted that at ISU "students usually are in smaller classes and do more expensive laboratory work."[29]

After all of the bitter argument and dramatics that had accompanied both cost studies and the Educational Load Factor, documentary history is remarkably empty of comment on this result. The closest thing I have discovered to a reaction by any of the principals is a letter from Hancher to Hilton and Maucker. Writing, of the cost study results, "I seriously question whether they should be used for any purpose other than internal analysis," Hancher's attempt to downplay their significance is rather vague and somehow halfhearted, compared with the debate of two years earlier.[30] His administration had then argued with much greater force that cost studies could offer only limited guidance as to "what should be," in budgeting. Perhaps, though, Hancher now sensed that any other arguments were undercut by what had been his most powerful message of all: *Either the cost figures are the true and correct costs of adding students to existing enrollments or they are not.* After four years' work, it seemed that they were. Despite all State University of Iowa's protests, furthermore, the rest of the Regents system seemed satisfied that this did supersede any claims by SUI of a unique burden.

For years President Hilton had insisted that an Educational Load Factor, if such existed, must apply to all schools and not just SUI. Hancher's administration had never quite found a convincing reason for claiming otherwise, but had pressed and pressed the disputed concept and ignored Hilton's pleas to work together on the basis of the old, unadjusted Toledo formula. In the end Hancher got exactly what he wished for and nothing like what he actually wanted. Two months later, it was probably one more reason he made such a dramatically ambitious budget request. He had won the argument's principle but lost its practical object, and with one last opportunity he asked for the result he had hoped to get from the Educational Load Factor, anyway.

In a limited sense, the board approved his request. The Regents ultimately cut SUI's proposed $6 million for strengthening programs to less than half that, but it was still a substantial award from an objective standpoint, and approximately twice their request on behalf of ISU for the same category.[31] Meanwhile, the appropriate role of cost findings remained undecided; SUI's concept of Educational Load Factor was essentially turned on its head, but in practice no proportionate shift of funds toward ISU followed.

In the end, the theorist Hancher who argued again and again for thinking about the long term had lost most of those arguments to the more pragmatic Hilton. But he had also closed his presidency with a series of short-term victories in the most practical competition of all. Considered this way it seemed that only time would reveal who, if anyone, had emerged as winner. The only thing certain in the summer of 1964 was that the fighting, itself, was done.

CHAPTER THIRTEEN
Legacies

Virgil Hancher's longevity in office was a mixed blessing for his immediate legacy. I imagine that, by his last year, there were at least a few undergraduates whose parents had his name on their own diplomas. All but one of the university's deans were Hancher appointees.[1] To nearly an entire generation he was the president and, in a sense, was the university. For that reason alone he was not going to depart without a fair measure of sentiment, even on the part of sometimes-adversaries. Iowa City businesses, some of whom had sued Hancher's administration to block plans for the Memorial Union hotel (without success), delivered a warm tribute via the Chamber of Commerce. The Board of Regents Hancher had castigated earlier in the year awarded him an honorary doctorate, as well as the formal title of President Emeritus.[2] Newspapers heaped praise upon Hancher's achievements and colleagues looked forward to his planned return to teach law, after a two-year appointment to the Ford Foundation.[3]

After a quarter-century, however, a change in leadership is nearly always perceived as "a breath of fresh air" whatever the merits of the old regime. Something of this effect seems to have muted esteem for the Hancher era then and since. The historian Stow Persons, whose career spanned the majority of Hancher's presidency and all of his successor Howard Bowen's, titled the pair's respective chapters in *The University of Iowa in the Twentieth Century* "The Inertial University" and "The Bowen Revival." Bowen was an economics professor, and the president of Grinnell College before the Regents' summons; he was younger and more in step with the times than the outgoing president, and more in step with academia than the dark horse Hancher had ever been. Most significant of all for his predecessor's legacy, he began immediately moving the university away from the battles to which Hancher had committed it.

Bowen consciously prioritized better relations within the Regents system, particularly with Iowa State University. He essentially forfeited Hancher's whole claim to liberal arts and humanities as any special preserve of State University of Iowa. The expansion of Iowa State and State College of Iowa, away from the special-purpose institutions Hancher had advocated, was of course underway already. Under President Bowen it ceased to be any source of real controversy. On funding, too, the new president preferred conciliation to competition. Bowen's administration made no attempt to pursue further Educational Load Factor awards—a task which might have been too much even for Hancher's stubbornness by that point—or to launch other claims to a larger budget than his peers would consider fair.

Those peers responded with enthusiasm. When the board and administrators emerged from closed-door discussions, the proposed budget for improving programs still included almost twice as much money for SUI as for Iowa State, as noted. Yet Hilton in particular seemed satisfied that his new counterpart's approach was a real, welcome difference. A month later he addressed returning staff ahead of his final school year, and at the same time looked back on several "amusing incidents" that had not been so entertaining at first. Most involved his running feud with President Hancher in one way or another, but the final item seemed present mostly as an acknowledgment that this was now done. If Hilton was in some way bemused to be "Cooperating with SUI," that experience was likely a pleasure from the very first.[4]

Even some outsiders got caught up in the seeming new spirit among Iowa's public colleges. Though journalists were excluded from the meetings where administrators settled on final budget requests, the sober *Des Moines Register* found afterward that "officials of the institutions were reported ready to face the Legislature with a one-for-all and all-for-one solidarity."[5] After years of loudly contested budget debates the change was simply obvious, and Bowen had been in office barely one month. For all the respect professed for President Hancher, people seemed agreed that quietly forgetting the controversies of his tenure was best for all concerned. Before the year was out, President Bowen proved that his desire to accommodate them was strong enough to court a small controversy of his own.

HANCHER VS. HILTON

Ever since the campaign to rename Iowa State College gained momentum in the late 1950s, some degree of controversy had hovered around names in the Regents system. Within that controversy, confusion proved the most lasting complaint. The addition of a second official university had not inaugurated this confusion, in fairness, but it had not helped the situation. Nor had Iowa State Teachers College's adoption of the name State College of Iowa, which eliminated the lone distinctive word found anywhere among the institutions. By 1963 the *Iowa City Press-Citizen* likely spoke for many in concluding that

> The problem... is a law—the one that says the State University of Iowa is at Iowa City, Iowa State University is at Ames and the State College of Iowa is at Cedar Falls. This may be clear to Iowans, although it's doubtful, but the plethora of "states," "Iowas," and "universities" seems to be just too much for those who don't deal with it frequently.[6]

The solution, in the view of the *Press-Citizen*'s editors, was one that various Iowans had proposed for decades, i.e. "a striking out of 'State' from the name of the University of Iowa."[7] The shorter name had enjoyed scattered informal use for decades, inside the university and out. As far back as 1918, one SUI official sought President Jessup's aid for his efforts, "for several years to accustom people to the name 'University of Iowa' in harmony with the nomenclature of practically all other great state universities."[8] But it never stuck. Perhaps the very fact that "State University of Iowa" was distinctive lent it an appeal. More significant was the fact that the State University in Iowa City was not named by "a law" but the Iowa Constitution itself. Even when Article IX Section 15 made obsolete the restriction to a single university at Iowa City, the new section introduced its own reference to "the State University."

For President Hancher, this had been effectively final. He did not propose to change Iowa's constitution, and probably had no wish to do so. His alternative ideas had been, variously, inviting the Regents to offer an idea of their own, or else folding all three institutions into a single university system. Potentially a reorganization into Iowa City, Ames and Cedar Falls campuses of a State University of Iowa system would have resolved the dilemma—but it found no more fans in 1964 than it had in 1959, and there the matter remained until Howard Bowen took office. Barely three months later, he introduced the solution that has prevailed since.

In a sense, Bowen's answer to the problem of two "State Universities" in Iowa was merely the obvious. The older, liberal arts university would conform to custom elsewhere and become "the University of Iowa." His response to the complexity of changing the formal name was equally straightforward: he ignored it. What was in the constitution could remain in the constitution, and on other legal documents. Everywhere else SUI would become the U of I. As Bowen reminded the Regents, he had already used much the same approach to the same problem at Grinnell. When its formal name "Iowa College" had seemed likely to be confused with the renamed State College of Iowa, President Bowen simply adopted the name of the surrounding town for practical use without going through any legal transition. That had worked out fine, and he saw no reason the same would not work for the University of Iowa. Rather than lobbying the legislature he suggested the Regents could approve the plan on their own, and on November 2, 1964 they did.[9]

At least one member of Iowa's legislature, however, took exception to being left out of the process. Presidents Hilton and Maucker had brought their pleas for new names before the General Assembly for its approval. Elmer F. Lange, of Sac City, apparently found it less than respectful for this brand-new president to conspire with the Regents in approving an equivalent action without consulting legislators at all. Practicing the respect for protocol that he found lacking, Lange asked Iowa's attorney general for a ruling. Though an alumnus who had attended the university during Hancher's presidency, Evan Hultman displayed no favoritism. After considering Lange's request for several weeks, Attorney General Hultman replied that he had been correct in questioning the matter: "The Board of Regents is an administrative body of express powers which do not include the power to change the name of the university at Iowa City."[10]

This apparently satisfied Rep. Lange, and the vexing issue of state university names and the Iowa Constitution ended there. The *Muscatine Journal* predicted in a headline that "Nobody's Going to Sue" and that proved the case.[11] Once more, most people seemed content that the new president would bend principles a little in order for everyone to coexist more easily.

What the old president thought of this, I can only guess; Hancher himself had bent the rules in the days of pre-auditing,

LEGACIES

but I imagine he may have seen this issue differently. If nothing else he must have regretted the reduction of State University of Iowa to a standard "University of" school, if only for what it symbolized. Perhaps he resigned himself to the new policies as merely acknowledging reality, but I don't imagine that he liked it. His dream for SUI had always been a kind of exceptionalism. Now that dream, or at least that form of it, was finished.

Hancher's thoughts were literally half a world away by the time President Bowen made his proposal to the Board of Regents. Just weeks after leaving office Hancher boarded a plane to India along with Mrs. Hancher. It was their second visit and, once again, something of a working getaway after a difficult period. In 1949 Hancher's attendance at an Indian-American Relations conference, to represent the Association of American Universities, may have been a welcome opportunity for renewal after attacks by legislators earlier in the year.[12] The experience also left a strong impression. Hancher reflected multiple times, afterward, on the poverty and possible future of the newly independent state. In considering his life after the presidency, the chance to check up on and perhaps make some contribution to India's development likely influenced his choice of an offer from the Ford Foundation. He planned to spend most of two years in India, as a consultant on higher education. Then, refreshed, he would return to Iowa with Mrs. Hancher and start a new chapter in life as a professor of law.

Newspapers suggested that Hancher would also be a consultant for his successor's administration in some capacity, and it's interesting to speculate on opinions and advice that he might have given President Bowen. Unfortunately, speculation and might-have-been are all that came of this. On January 30, 1965, Virgil Hancher died in a New Delhi hospital following a heart attack. His wife Susan, by his side at the end[13], would return the late president to Iowa for burial rather than a new beginning.

Hancher's death was a shock to all. After his mild heart attack nine years earlier, he had apparently recovered completely. Friends spoke of the president looking genuinely younger in his 60s than the decade before[14], and like Hancher himself they had every expectation of a long, productive third act to his career. Instead the thoughtful, reflective president emeritus was denied a chance to reflect on his own achievements at any length. Assessing his presidency and his life was left to others.

The surprise may have been such that not everyone was ready for even a first-draft statement. Hancher's old champion Earl Hall was deeply wounded by the loss, but managed to lead off formal eulogies with a moving tribute to his friend and peer. The announcement in the *Des Moines Register*, by contrast, seemed to struggle with capturing some personal sense of Hancher; though it only accompanied an inside continuation of the story, and was presumably well-intentioned, I still wince at the choice of "Student Driving Habits Irked Him" as heading. At the same time though, I like to think that someone at the paper demonstrated instincts that made up for it by going promptly to President Hilton for comment. Hilton's reaction appeared on the front page of the local section, well above that of President Bowen. This seems fitting. If any person could have offered an immediate and relevant comment on the public life that made Hancher's death newsworthy, it was Hilton.

LEGACIES

The two men were of similar age; they had occupied closely related positions, which would define their legacies, in parallel; they had, of course, fought together and against one another for much of a decade.

Hilton's comment itself was fitting, as well. His summary of his rival was typically simple and unequivocal: "Virgil Hancher will be remembered as one of the great presidents of the University of Iowa. He was one of the state's most able and effective educational leaders for a quarter of a century."[15]

When Hilton left the presidency of Iowa State five months later, reaction was equally positive, and equally firm. As they had for Hancher, plaudits for the departing president poured forth. Newspapers counted up growth under Hilton in enrollments, and programs, and buildings. Colleagues praised him as a person and an administrator and looked forward to further involvement with the university, in Hilton's case to coordinate various departments' efforts to complete the Iowa State Center. Students presented him with a new Oldsmobile.[16]

Unlike Hancher, enthusiasm for Hilton's achievements was also as much forward-looking as backward-looking. Iowa State's new president was committed to the goals for which Hilton had fought, as much if not more so than his predecessor. Robert Parks had shared in those fights for years, already. He had pressed for renaming Iowa State College, and eagerly supported the expanded curriculum and new degrees to make it not just a university but a broad-based university.[17] Hilton, in turn, left no doubt that he supported the new administration on policy as well as personally. Upon splitting up the duties of provost in 1961 between two vice presidents, Hilton had promoted Parks to vice president of academic affairs. In doing so he positioned Parks as his intended successor[18], and the Board of Regents proved happy to endorse the choice. Just as it had at the University of Iowa, the new administration was arguably the most meaningful verdict on the old one. At Iowa State, however, that verdict was not just *well done*, but solidly *let's keep going*.

Hilton shared the same spirit. After reviewing highs and lows of his presidency at his final faculty convocation, he confessed that "The best way I can describe the past eleven years is to say that they have been rough, tough, exciting, glorious years" and that he felt quite ready to relinquish the duties of the president. But he was not planning to retire from the mission. His expected his new role to be a full-time job, and pledged that "I hope to spend the rest of my life working for Iowa State."[19]

In the event this proved one of the few hopes that James Hilton did not realize at ISU. The following winter, he had a change of heart. It seemed that his loyalties were divided, after all, but no one at Iowa State was resentful. They had taken "Dr. Jimmie" from North Carolina in the first place and benefitted enormously; now, he wanted to return to his roots, and though sad to see him go Iowans couldn't complain. North Carolinians were his family first, as well as a second time when the Hiltons' children were putting down roots of their own. Formally Hilton was taking a job with a private foundation, in this case the Z. Smith Reynolds Foundation based in Winston-Salem. But the roles of "dad" and "granddad" were likely as much on his mind in saying farewell.

LEGACIES

Even then he said that leaving was difficult. "The staff, students and alumni of the university, and the people of Iowa, have been wonderful to us," Hilton said, "But our major responsibilities here are about completed."[20] They would be fully completed one way or another, too, he added. Almost 14 years earlier he had insisted "I am quite determined about this Center,"[21] when it seemed an impossible fantasy. Now, though still unbuilt, the Iowa State Center had plans, organization, money, and momentum that was unlikely to falter. Hilton still remained ready to hunt for every last penny until concrete set and doors opened.

Doors to the Iowa State Center began opening on September 13, 1969.[22] A series of concerts by the New York Philharmonic welcomed the first audiences to C.Y. Stephens Auditorium, named for a campaign chair and major donor. The high caliber of the Center's opening performance set a tone for what followed. Compared with the makeshift spaces which Stephens and subsequent components replaced, "the udder university" vaulted into the ranks of significant sites for the arts. President Parks's biographer Robert Underhill notes that Stephens "immediately became a magnet, attracting performing artists otherwise not seen in Iowa or perhaps anywhere in the Midwest."[23]

More success followed. The "large coliseum" took another two years to complete, partly by intent. Both Hilton and Parks viewed the arts as the Center's top priority[24], and while its largest component has hosted concerts, as well as commencement ceremonies, it was first and foremost a space for athletic contests. The first of these played at the Iowa State Center ended well, also. On December 2, 1971, the Cyclones defeated the University of Arizona for a 71-54 men's basketball victory.

In the long run, the outcome of this "housewarming" would prove less memorable than that of the building's formal dedication ceremony. Several months earlier, President Parks revealed that the great concrete monument would be named for the Iowa State Center's ultimate architect: James H. Hilton Coliseum.[25]

Hilton himself was back in Iowa for the occasion. His presence and the naming itself were appropriate recognition for his efforts. In a small way, the same might be said of another reception for the Iowa State Center, rumored to be less adulatory. James G. Hilton recalls that some in Iowa resented the

James H. Hilton, outside of Hilton Coliseum.
University Photographs, Box 65, Iowa State University Library Special Collections.

LEGACIES

Center at first, for leapfrogging what has traditionally been the state's flagship university.[26] Although such a reaction might not be formally recorded, it could have occurred. If so it's somehow fitting that in his most obvious, material legacy, Hilton offended views of the University of Iowa's prerogative one last time.

Any bitterness was short-lived, all the same. Though the auditorium which Hancher had called for since the 1940s took until 1972 to open, it did at least prove worth the wait. Over the years, Hancher Auditorium won its own share of critical acclaim and headline performances. Prominent music critic Byron Belt attended opening ceremonies, and declared the auditorium "worthy of the greatest cultural center anywhere."[27] More recently, a columnist for the *Iowa City Press-Citizen* memorialized it as "one of University of Iowa's best-known and most beloved facilities,"[28] after floods forced its closure in 2008. By that time, "Hancher" had in a sense outgrown the building anyway, becoming a performing arts organization that kept the name and mission alive. Somewhat remarkably, in an era when "naming rights" are a major source of capital funds, the grand new auditorium opened in 2016 preserves the Hancher name as well.

Both Hancher and Hilton could be justly proud of the physical reminders of their efforts. Only one, of course, was privileged to see them. James Hilton enjoyed just the sort of long, satisfying retirement denied his rival. He basked in recognition of his achievements at Iowa State, and recorded his own thoughts in a brief but lively memoir. He found a productive second career,

HANCHER VS. HILTON

The original Hancher auditorium (like Hilton Coliseum) proved vulnerable to flooding. After a severe flood in 2008, the university closed and eventually replaced it.

Photo by Daniel Hartwig.

The new Hancher Auditorium, opened in 2016.

not only evaluating grants for the Reynolds Foundation[29] but chairing a public education study which would have interested Hancher greatly, at the request of North Carolina's governor. He also naturally found more time for his family, although this included the one great disappointment in otherwise golden years. In 1969, Lois Hilton died of cancer[30] without seeing any of the monuments to her partner or their lasting impact on central Iowa, which had been her first home.

In time, though, the septuagenarian James Hilton married again. As with his first marriage, he owed Iowa State for introducing him to his betrothed. In 1970 Hilton wed Helen LeBaron, who had fought her own inter-institutional battles as dean of home economics. LeBaron's long tenure as dean was not yet over, either, and though married in North Carolina the new Mr. and Mrs. Hilton made their home in Ames.

Unlike his spouse, James Hilton soon settled into a fuller retirement. Both of them also returned often to North Carolina, for lengthy visits. Nonetheless Dr. Hilton did, except for the three years before his remarriage, spend the rest of what proved a long life around Iowa State after all.

CHAPTER FOURTEEN
Evaluation

In February 1989, a journalist named John Turnbull inadvertently created one of Iowa State University's best-known traditions. In previewing a men's basketball match-up with the third-ranked Missouri Tigers, he suggested that "the magic of Hilton Coliseum" might give the Cyclones a fighting chance.[1] The phrase caught the eye of an editor at the *Des Moines Register* who included it in the story's headline. With that, and the Iowa State win that followed, Hilton Magic gradually took on a life of its own. When Hilton Coliseum hosted ESPN's *College GameDay* in 2015, the network's Jay Williams said that "I think [*GameDay*] needs to go to the best atmosphere... I've heard so much about the magic of Hilton Coliseum."[2] For Iowa State fans, this particular "magic" is now so inseparable from Cyclone basketball that the Sprint Center in Kansas City is regarded as "Hilton South."

This might at least have amused James H. Hilton, had he witnessed it. The former president died seven years before

HANCHER VS. HILTON

Turnbull's moment of inspiration, however, at the ripe old age of 82. Thus he missed entirely his name's surprising rise to national, if specialized, recognition in the 21st century.

I doubt that this would have bothered Hilton much. Ever appreciative of the Iowa State community's support, he would no doubt have accepted the strange honor with sincere thanks. But Hilton regarded other accomplishments as more important than the entire Iowa State Center, in addition to seeing the coliseum as a secondary priority even within it. This lasting, formal recognition of his accomplishments is still deserved and commendable, as it is with Virgil Hancher and his own curiously twinned monument. It just may be fitting in an even deeper sense. But in any direct sense, the most obvious legacies of Hancher and Hilton are still coincidental to their lives and labors and arguments. Any true assessment of what these mean must, certainly, be about more than two buildings, or even all the physical impact on their respective institutions combined.

In which case, the question deserves consideration: what was it all about? What are we to make, 50 years later, of Hancher, Hilton and their battles?

For Hilton, I believe the answer is relatively simple. To a great extent it was already written out long ago on a single page now in his archives, in fact. Some time after Hilton's retirement, his information service chief Ned Disque appended a brief observation to a brochure promoting the "Iowa State College Ten Years From Now" agenda from 1955: "President Hilton had this piece prepared early in his administration. It essentially was all accomplished on schedule."[3] Arriving from

EVALUATION

North Carolina, Hilton drafted a long-range plan in consultation with leaders and constituencies whose support he would need, then kept working year in and year out to complete it. Eventually he marked the list as done, and returned to North Carolina once more.

The means by which Hilton accomplished his agenda are slightly more complicated. His personal style and career experience helped, certainly, as did chance. He had the good fortune to complete his tenure as president without a world war interrupting. He did, however, encounter challenges to his agenda more than once. I believe that over the long run, the simplicity and directness of his plans were key to bringing them past obstacles to a satisfying outcome.

In studying Hilton's career alongside that of his most frequent opponent, the concept of a "Zen" approach has occurred to me repeatedly. I debated the term for some time; Hilton was by no means unconcerned with larger ideas, and it would caricature his presidency to imply that he was nothing more than an efficient foreman. Yet he did have a gift for judging the material available to him and estimating precisely how much he might achieve with it. His close colleague Robert Parks observed the same aptitude and admired it in summing up his leadership; in Parks's words, Hilton had a remarkable "feeling for the possible" and instinct for "what can be accomplished."[4] Along with this, he suggested, Hilton's effectiveness was largely the product of tolerance, patience and infectious optimism.

Parks's assessment strikes me as insightful. It's a very plausible explanation for Hilton's success, but it feels even more compelling as an explanation for the contrasting results of his rival. Here, arguably, is an enumeration of all the most notable strengths that did not characterize Virgil Hancher. Thoughtful as well as intelligent and erudite, Hancher's patience was sorely tested by those who weren't. The large number of people fitting that description, and his institution's dependence on them, left him little optimism to share even if his powers of persuasion were suited to the task. Above all, whether the result of personal shortcomings or simple misfortune, Hancher's sense of which battles to fight was decidedly unreliable.

Virgil Hancher's presidency was bigger than his contests with Hilton, of course, and assessing the whole is more difficult. Historian Stow Persons sneered that Hancher "considered among his principal achievements during a presidency of twenty-four years the adoption of a funded faculty retirement system and a plan for medical faculty compensation,"[5] but I believe Persons's judgment is unfair. Saving a medical college from disintegration seems a worthy object of pride, even for an extended term of office. It's also worth noting that Hilton, whom Persons held up as a much more dynamic leader, had a remarkably similar view of his own achievements. In his own words Hilton's greatest satisfaction as president was "getting from the Legislature the necessary funds needed to improve salaries, insurance programs and retirement programs."[6] Given this, Hilton's positive comments on Hancher's presidency as a whole seem both sincere and reasonable. Such emphasis on the positive is, at the same time, one of the very qualities which Hancher lacked, and his contrasting attitude led him into many of the battles where his efforts were most disappointed.

In various musings on humanity, on spirituality, on contemplation itself there is something of a mystic character to Hancher. For all Hilton's depth, there were subjects among

EVALUATION

which Hancher ranged that Iowa State's president never explored, or at least not in public conversation. But if a mysticism did characterize Hancher it was not a Zen mysticism. Hancher was an exceptional thinker and a thinker of ambition, as well as depth—but he was also an exceptional worrier. To my own mind, he had reason to be. Virgil Hancher lived through two world wars, a deadly pandemic, the Great Depression and the advent of nuclear arms, in addition to an ongoing decline of Iowa's relative political and economic status, plus most of two decades in which its leadership was often indifferent to higher education's goals when not outright hostile. Given these experiences, Hancher's pessimism seems easy to understand. It was probably not, however, well-suited to the job he faced. If Hilton's optimism was less than completely rational, the same is true of human beings and our institutions. If Hancher's criticisms and suggestions regarding higher education were more thought-provoking than Hilton's 10-year plan, they were also more difficult to explain to a bureaucracy that instinctively tabled nearly any proposal that raised questions.

In rivalry with Hilton, Hancher's greatest successes were also his most obvious departures from habit; in making relatively simple claims that State University of Iowa deserved more money, he swayed the Board of Regents in his favor for a time. Otherwise his ambitions for what ought to be achieved were wide of the mark, compared with Hilton's conviction of what could be achieved. If President Hilton's approach was narrower, it was also laser-like. Hancher's, by contrast, was often that of a man with a lantern, investigating murky depths of philosophy. The effort was bold, and instructive, but of small attraction to most people who prefer a straight well-lit path.

HANCHER VS. HILTON

Differences in temperament and approach, it seems likely, help explain the results of Hancher's and Hilton's arguments. I believe they're also necessary to explain why the two presidents fought so many times, in spite of all their common interests. For whatever my opinion about the personal feelings of individuals I have never met may be worth, I've concluded that above and beyond policy arguments, President Hancher did simply dislike President Hilton.

There were multiple causes of friction between the two presidents, besides the specific debates that grew heated more and more swiftly. Their institutions had to some extent been rivals since their foundation. David Hamilton, a University of Kentucky professor with personal and professional connections to Iowa State, notes that most states with multiple public universities experience occasional competition; he recalls a resentful mood at his employer toward the University of Louisville, during the 1980s.[7] Around the time Hilton took office, nationwide trends left Iowa State with a choice of fully embracing the identity of a university, or else becoming an anachronism. Much of Hilton's agenda fit with the choice of a university, anyway, as did much of the institution even before his arrival—as the Association of American Universities acknowledged—but its formal status as a "college" had probably held back resentment by State University of Iowa. Abandoning that weakened the relatively settled peace that prevailed since the Board of Education's early years. At the same time, the combination of deferred capital investment and approaching record enrollments encouraged Hancher's administration to

EVALUATION

see appropriations as a zero-sum contest, and to see Hilton's agenda as threatening their already dissatisfactory share.

As valid as these factors are, however, they seem inadequate. The intensity of the Hancher-Hilton conflicts seems to demand something more, particularly because that intensity grew, steadily, during years when on balance the appropriations pie was also growing. On this, Hilton and Hancher were agreed: budgets invariably fell short of their requests but they were increasing significantly, relative to years of underfunding. A retrospective published by SUI late in Hancher's presidency acknowledged that "In 1957 and 1959, the Iowa General Assembly's bills for the support of University salaries and operating funds did much to overcome the cumulative lags of the post-war years."[8] In his own memoir, Hilton wrote that "both State and Federal funds were available during the years 1953 to 1965" in more liberal amounts than the years after he left office.[9] Even the pessimistic Hancher said in his final faculty meeting that, after the difficult relations with legislators during much of his time in office, "Trust and confidence began to supplant doubt and suspicion."[10] Yet relations between SUI and Iowa State grew worse during the years of bounty and trust, only to recover afterward.

Even with other pressures in effect, this implies something more than a competition for resources. Part of that something was, probably, personal enmity on Hancher's part. I was slow to accept this claim, despite both Hamilton and Stow Persons endorsing it. The former also suggests that Hilton "detested" Hancher in return, and here I still find room for doubt. As the longtime spouse of President Parks's daughter, Professor Hamilton is as near as anyone living to being an inside source on the Hilton administration. He cites family conversations in writing that "Hilton so disliked Hancher that he would not allow Iowa State officials to take rooms at Iowa's student union when the Board of Regents met in Iowa City."[11] But the controversial hotel facilities in the Iowa Memorial Union did not actually open until July 1965.[12] It's entirely possible that some time before then, Hilton commanded Parks and other staff to foreswear ever lodging with the university; in his reaction to Hancher's 1964 proposal to absorb ISU Extension, Hilton does appear angry enough that such a comment is plausible.

All the same, I am inclined to suspect that in Hilton's case anger did not harden into animosity. Aside from his son's remarks there are Hilton's own to consider. It's natural enough that, immediately upon learning of Hancher's unexpected death, Hilton was complimentary. Yet writing a decade later, in a memoir that has never been published, Hilton's comments were much the same. Acknowledging Hancher's opposition to many of his plans, Hilton declared that "He was an extremely able and very sensitive person. Personally I had a great admiration for him and I felt he did a great job for the University of Iowa."[13] The fact that Hilton also mentioned Hancher's status as a Rhodes scholar suggests to me that his respect for his rival was real, even if Robert Parks formed a different impression. I am considerably more convinced that this respect was not, however, reciprocated.

In an earlier chapter I wrote that formal archives are an unlikely place to store disparaging, personal views about a notable colleague, and to all appearances neither Hilton nor Hancher did so. But on one occasion Hancher at least came very close. Near the end of his presidency, he composed a rambling seven-

EVALUATION

page survey of dissatisfactions with the Regents system, large and small. Along with restating his case for a university system, the text includes bitter complaints of underhanded conduct by State College of Iowa and, particularly, Iowa State. Strangest of all, Hancher's most furious criticism is directed at planned new dormitories at ISU. The SUI president seemed convinced that the proposed construction was both excessive and at the same time of such low standard as verged on criminal. "Do the Regents," he asked, "want to be a party to what may be a virtual fraud on the bondholders?"[14]

The entire document, in fairness, has the character of a private catharsis. At one point Hancher indulges a tangent criticizing American dormitories, generally, as the root of all student misbehavior and arguing that shared-occupancy rooms are a menace to social order. Most likely the majority of the content was never sent to anyone. The first page is labeled "DRAFT," and it's unclear who, if anyone, was its intended audience. This, though, seems all the more reason to consider that it does offer a glimpse of Hancher's private opinions, the implications of which are unmistakably negative toward James Hilton. Though Hancher did not mention Hilton by name, his comments are a judgment on Hilton as both an administrator and a person. In Hancher's assessment Iowa State's actions had been unfair, ungentlemanly, and even fraudulent; it's difficult to imagine that Hancher retained any personal esteem for Iowa State's president. Even if the text is an exaggerated version of Hancher's feelings, written in anger, the underlying sentiment was likely real. Unlike Hancher's objection to admitting Iowa State to the AAU, nothing in his other words or deeds meaningfully contradicts this later instance of antipathy.

One other anecdote about Hancher seems worth mentioning as an instance of relatively favorable opinion about Iowa State, which nonetheless reinforces the impression of personal disdain for James Hilton. According to Professor Hamilton, "[Robert] Parks got along well with Hancher and Hancher was immensely pleased when he was named Iowa State's president."[15] This feels credible, not least because to some extent I expected it even before contacting Hamilton. In many ways Parks seems much more naturally aligned with Hancher. Parks shared the SUI president's esteem for liberal arts and humanities; unlike Hilton, he had made it his own field, earning multiple degrees in political science. The two even shared a similar appearance of archetypal, thoughtful scholarly refinement. If only for the sake of argument it does seem worth considering that Hancher was in fact favorably inclined to Parks as president. Yet if so, it seems difficult to avoid suspecting that Hancher was correspondingly repelled by Hilton, because Parks shared essentially the same agenda for Iowa State.

Parks revered the liberal arts tradition, but also wanted to expand it at what Hancher believed should be a special-purpose technical institute. Parks did just that as president, adding new degrees even more enthusiastically than his predecessor. Likewise, it was Parks who actively encouraged a reluctant Hilton in campaigning for the name Iowa State University.

Given Parks's commitment to exactly those policies that the SUI president consistently opposed, Persons's claim that Hancher simply hated Hilton seems confirmed if Hancher's approval of Parks can be believed. For my own part, I can believe it, though I also believe that it speaks less of bias on Hancher's part than of a generally more choleric temperament.

EVALUATION

Hancher's wariness of Iowa State predated Hilton's presidency, and as years passed it extended to State College of Iowa in large measure. Therefore if Hancher did come to detest Hilton personally, I propose that policy differences still contributed more to personal differences than vice versa. Quite possibly Hancher would have grown just as resentful of a Parks presidency had he confronted one. As it happened he never did, and if Hancher held a favorable view of the prospect after he left office, that doesn't necessarily make his lower estimate of Hilton a character flaw. It just reminds us that Hancher was human.

Whether policy arguments drove a personal component to Hancher and Hilton's feud, or merely exacerbated it, those arguments' substance invites some kind of audit as well. In terms of whose policies prevailed, in his own time Hilton was essentially on the winning side and Hancher the losing side, almost invariably. But Hancher warned of long-term consequences as much as immediate priorities. Fifty years later, it ought to be possible to say something about who should have won, as well as who did.

If I have refrained from judging this issue earlier, however, it is not solely from reluctance to get ahead of my narrative. Some of Hancher's and Hilton's debates were enormously complex. It's possible that a dozen entirely neutral experts on finance and accounting and college administration might be able to review the Educational Load Factor controversy, with the benefit of hindsight and modern information technology, and reach an unimpeachable conclusion as to whether or not the concept ever made sense and whom it should have benefitted, if so. Yet it's unlikely that any such experts, let alone those with no attachment to Iowa or its colleges, will ever do so.

Meanwhile, the distance of decades also complicates questions that were simpler, in their initial context, because so much has changed. The entire field of home economics as a college-level subject has largely gone into eclipse; modern references to "vocational home economics" are almost nonexistent. Nuclear engineering remains more relevant, but the future of ubiquitous nuclear power envisioned at mid-century has proved mostly illusory, and the University of Iowa discontinued its efforts in the field decades ago. Extension still exists, but seems less likely to spark a war than ever. The U of I program long ago disappeared under the heading "continuing education." Based on my own experience, one can grow up in a relatively rural part of Iowa, and graduate from Iowa State, with only the faintest awareness of its own service.

With so much changed since these programs were fiercely contested controversies, the most reliable conclusions about the disputes of that era may involve what hasn't happened. Contrary to President Hancher's repeated fears, I feel safe in suggesting that disaster has not befallen the University of Iowa. The state of Iowa authorized a second university, then a third within the following decade. If neither one operates a complete "duplicate liberal arts college" in name, both come close in function. In the 21st century Iowa State offers multiple humanities degrees that even Hilton promised it would respect as the University of Iowa's preserve. Despite all of which, the sky has not fallen.

EVALUATION

Skepticism attaches to college rankings as firmly today as in 1965, or for that matter 1925. It sometimes appears that no college can fail to find some recognition of which to boast. If that is possible, though, none of Iowa's Regents universities have sunk so low. In 2011 *Washington Monthly* ranked Iowa State above the California Institute of Technology, while recent years have seen the University of Iowa reliably around number 72 out of all the institutions surveyed by *US News & World Report.* Meanwhile, if Hancher might still perceive mediocrity in satisfaction at this accomplishment, it's worth considering that elite status is inherently relative. If many of America's universities attract students from around the world, it still seems fair to suggest some evidence of quality in the fact that Iowa's are among those universities. My own degree program of graphic design—a rather tiny department and by no means an aggressively promoted flagship—included three international students in my graduating class alone.

At the same time, it's worth asking whether Hancher's vision would have made much difference. In 1960 the total enrollment of SUI, ISU and ISTC was around 27,000; today over 70,000 students attend the Regents universities. Concentrating resources on a smaller, single university might have resulted in more of an elite institution. But Hancher never offered a convincing explanation of how this restriction would work within his concept of accessible public higher education.

Given the scale of the numbers, it seems unlikely that a single university enrolling all 70,000 students would offer significantly better value than three universities, two of which are now larger than the entire Regents system was in Hancher's day. On that basis his alternate proposal for a university system seems even less promising. Judged objectively, this was not the sinister power-grab that loyalists of the other schools might perceive, nor was it politically unreasonable. Other states consolidated public colleges and universities around the same time or even later. Nonetheless, the evidence that this produces a significantly greater efficiency is distinctly lacking. A number of states have university systems. But some have more than one, while Iowa is by no means alone in maintaining multiple, relatively independent universities. Taken as a whole, the bewildering variety among America's 50 states suggests that no real "best practice" has yet emerged in this regard.

Hancher's underlying conviction that specialization would resolve the dilemma of access and quality has not fared especially well, either. The notion was already in some doubt well before he became president. The Capen report of 1925, one of the series commissioned by the Board of Education over the years, noted that even then "Combined enrollments were four times what they had been ten years earlier, and the increased size tended to minimize the cost of operating separate institutions."[16] Realistically, many subjects offer little in the way of economies of scale. Metallurgy or nuclear medicine programs may require expensive machines that can serve quite a large number of students before two of a given machine are necessary—but one English department of 600 students offers little obvious potential for lower expenses than two departments of 300. Cheap information technology has probably reduced the number of programs to which "duplication" is genuinely relevant even further, at the same time as overall enrollment sets new records.

EVALUATION

In the long run Iowa's universities seem to have preserved the most specialized, technical or professional subjects as single programs, despite the incentives for mimicry and expansion that Hancher feared would be unchecked without more centralized control. Iowa State has not entered the fields of law, or medicine, or dentistry, and the University of Iowa leaves agriculture and (most) engineering to ISU. Otherwise, duplication has essentially ceased to be controversial. Hancher's suspicion that state colleges' demand for liberal arts degrees might prove a "fad" has failed to pan out; today even his model for special-purpose focus, MIT, offers programs in political science, literature, and women's and gender studies.[17] The Board of Regents' policies still include a formal statement against duplication[18], yet in practice it seems largely perfunctory. The chair of the Iowa Senate's education committee recalls no serious discussion of duplication more recent than 25 years ago.[19] Given the contrasting obsession with the issue which characterized much of Hancher's presidency, it's understandable that he failed to predict this. Nonetheless in echoing the era's crusade against duplication, it was in hindsight Hancher himself who joined in a passing fad.

Perhaps the best thing that can be said of Virgil Hancher's warnings about the future of public college is that, if they weren't right, they weren't entirely wrong either. Hilton was by most measures correct that more than one broad-based university in Iowa would be viable. But Hancher was equally correct in warning that state appropriations would never meet their costs. In the 21st century the concept of the low-tuition public college, predominantly funded by the state treasury, is perhaps more archaic than any other feature of Hancher's and Hilton's era.

In truth, the erosion of this model had been well underway even then. It turned out that the years of catching up during Hilton's administration were the anomaly, rather than the decades of lean funds that preceded them. The pessimist Hancher was right to fear this, even if he erred in forecasting that his proposed reforms represented the solution. The solution, as such, has instead proved to be a combination of what he and Hilton regarded as limited, subsidiary resources explored out of necessity—higher tuition, and aggressive fundraising—combined with federal loans and grants.

Traditionalist as he generally was, Hancher probably would not have felt that this outcome vindicated an optimist's view. Notably, neither did Hilton. Writing in the 1970s, Hilton was able to look back and conclude that for all of his rapport with legislators, he had also been president in a period that was simply, "by accident perhaps, the best period in the long history of the Land-Grant college system to be a chief administrator in such an educational institution." Noting the waning of public support since, the closing lines of Hilton's retrospective recall the speeches and memos and letters of his old rival. Hilton perceived a public disenchanted with public education's rising price tag and with land-grant institutions' drift from some of their traditional emphases. He even saw competition from new technical and community colleges as diluting such money as taxpayers did provide.[20]

One could claim this as a partial vindication for Hancher, certainly, and given the generosity to his old rival elsewhere

EVALUATION

in his memoir, Hilton probably would have been the last to object. Yet it also, I suspect, simply demonstrates one of the inherent features of rivalries: genuine rivals are necessarily contemporaries, and time's passage inevitably magnifies the similarities of such pairings even as their differences tend to grow obscure. Some degree of rivalry between the University of Iowa and Iowa State continues, and recent debate over funding formulae has even brought back some taste of the 1960s' competition. But I doubt that the modern U of I community particularly resents that Iowa State is called a university, and teaches English as a major rather than a service course; even if the University of Iowa still taught vocational home economics, Iowa State's most die-hard partisans probably wouldn't care.

Meanwhile, for all that they disagreed about how to slice it, Hilton and Hancher were united in believing that the state's portion of public universities' cost should grow, not diminish. For all that they disagreed about how and where to teach it, they shared not only enthusiasm for liberal arts and humanities education but a reasoning that now seems almost utopian. As often as they argued with one another, both men argued even more passionately that higher education needed to impart an understanding of human society, and an interest in how technological innovation impacts the life of all, not just that of its elite masters. Though today's leaders might well agree, my personal impression is that this commitment has in practice become nearly as vestigial as reducing duplication.

If both Hancher and Hilton could reappear today, they would likely have a far stronger opinion on all of this. Perhaps, if they could speak to us once more, they might offer a united and compelling reminder of values that seem lost, as college education has become more a basic credential for personal enrichment, and less a project of society for improving society. Their dialogue, impassioned and challenging if sometimes acrimonious, is denied such a conclusion, however. Any further progress toward their core, shared goals must depend on our considering its reminders, and deciding for ourselves whether there is wisdom yet to be learned from two remarkable educators.

ACKNOWLEDGEMENTS

I want to thank James G. Hilton for his generosity in answering my questions, examining my manuscript and offering so much encouragement. It was a true honor to speak with him.

The Special Collections departments at both Iowa State and the University of Iowa were consistently welcoming and helpful in my research. Particular thanks to David McCartney at the U of I for assistance with a number of obscure questions.

I am also grateful to Professor David Hamilton, and Josh Lehman at the Iowa Board of Regents, for their patient correspondence.

Finally, thanks to Joan Husmann for sharp-eyed work editing and proofreading.

SELECT BIBLIOGRAPHY

Virgil Hancher and James Hilton are the subject of a large number of published works, but the majority of these are relatively brief articles. Many of these are cited in the notes which follow. Their schools' most recent official histories are both useful and interesting, as is Robert Underhill's biography of Robert Parks, who served in Hilton's administration. Gerald Peterson's essay on the University of Northern Iowa's history is also worth highlighting, for its third-party perspective on the controversies among Iowa's public colleges.

Stow Persons, *The University of Iowa in the Twentieth Century: An Institutional History* (Iowa City: University of Iowa Press, 1990).

Robert Underhill, *Alone Among Friends: A Biography of W. Robert Parks* (Ames: Iowa State University Press, 1999).

A Sesquicentennial History of Iowa State University: Tradition and Transformation, ed. Dorothy Schweider and Gretchen Van Houten (Ames: Iowa State University Press, 2007).

Gerald L. Peterson, "Brief History of UNI, 1876-1995," University of Northern Iowa Rod Library, last modified January 28, 2016, https://www.library.uni.edu/collections/special-collections/university-archives/brief-history-uni-1876-1995

James Hilton's memoir, as close to a biography of either president as exists, is an invaluable treasure. Unfortunately it remains unpublished, although a copy is stored at the Ames library's Heritage Room in addition to the typescript in Hilton's papers. A sketch prepared by University of Iowa staff is the nearest approximation to a Hancher biography. His faculty file contains a typescript of this, as well as two published versions from 1960.

James H. Hilton, "James. H. Hilton's Story from 1899-1965," Hilton papers box 1, folder 4.

"Virgil M. Hancher," typescript biography, c. 1960, Virgil M. Hancher Faculty Vertical File, folder 1.

"In Honor of President and Mrs. Virgil M. Hancher of the University of Iowa," dinner program, April 20, 1960, Virgil M. Hancher Faculty Vertical File, folder 2.

"The President and the University: 1940-60," *Iowa Alumni Review*, June 1960, Virgil M. Hancher Faculty Vertical File, folder 2.

For comprehensive study, there is no substitute for examining the two presidents' papers. Among Hilton's papers, individual labels on most folders are generally helpful, and the Iowa State library's web site provides a list of these (http://www.add.lib.iastate.edu/spcl/arch/rgrp/02-10.pdf). Hancher left behind a

SELECT BIBLIOGRAPHY

much larger archive, reflecting a presidency of nearly 25 years. His papers are also more complex to search, although library staff are consistently helpful. Fortunately the three large folders of Hancher's faculty file offer a very accessible introduction to his career.

James H. Hilton Papers, RS 2/10, Special Collections Department, Iowa State University Library.

Virgil M. Hancher Faculty Vertical File. Faculty and Staff Vertical Files Records [RG01.0015.003], The University of Iowa Libraries, Iowa City, Iowa.

Virgil M. Hancher Papers [RG05.0001.011], The University of Iowa Libraries, Iowa City, Iowa.

NOTES

INTRODUCTION

1. C.W. De Kiewiet to Virgil Hancher, c. February 1958, box 1.16 folder "De Kiewiet article," Association of American Universities Records Ms. 197, Special Collections, Milton S. Eisenhower Library, The Johns Hopkins University.

2. Bob Henry, The 10 O'Clock News script, KCRG-TV (Cedar Rapids, Iowa) January 29, 1964, box 13 folder 71, James H. Hilton Papers, RS 2/10, Special Collections Department, Iowa State University Library.

3. Virgil M. Hancher, "Hancher Looks at Future of University of Iowa," *Cedar Rapids Gazette*, February 2, 1964.

4. United Press International, untitled wire story, January 29, 1964, Hilton papers box 13, folder 71.

5. Frank Deford, "Frank Deford Cheers on Underdog, State University," Morning Edition, NPR, November 20, 2002, http://www.npr.org/templates/story/story.php?storyId=849783

6. Stow Persons, *The University of Iowa in the Twentieth Century: An Institutional History* (Iowa City: University of Iowa Press, 1990).

7. David Hamilton, "Science with Humanity: The Parks Years," in *A Sesquicentennial History of Iowa State University: Tradition and Transformation*, ed. Dorothy Schweider and Gretchen Van Houten (Ames: Iowa State University Press, 2007).

CHAPTER 1

1. Frank H. Uriell, A Tribute by Frank H. Uriell (pamphlet reprinting from Summer 1964 *Iowa Law Review*), folder 2, Virgil M. Hancher Faculty Vertical File, Faculty and Staff Vertical Files Records, The University of Iowa Libraries, Iowa City, Iowa.

2. Pete Hoyt, "Would Rescind Hancher Election," *Cedar Rapids Gazette*, October 21, 1940.

3. Stow Persons, *The University of Iowa in the Twentieth Century: An Institutional History* (Iowa City: University of Iowa Press, 1990).

4. "The President and the University: 1940-60," *Iowa Alumni Review*, June 1960, 4.
5. "Inaugural Address by Dr. Hancher," *Mount Pleasant News*, May 4, 1950.
6. Virgil M. Hancher, "Reminiscences," *Iowa Alumni Review*, June 1964, 5.
7. W. Earl Hall, "The President: My Friend," *Iowa Alumni Review*, June 1960, 10.
8. Virgil M. Hancher, "Reminiscences," *Iowa Alumni Review*, June 1964, 5.
9. Frank H. Uriell, A Tribute by Frank H. Uriell (pamphlet reprinting from Summer 1964 *Iowa Law Review*), Hancher Faculty Vertical File folder 2.
10. "44-Year-Old Chicago Attorney; Alumnus of University, Named," *Iowa City Press-Citizen*, September 9, 1940.
11. Virgil M. Hancher to Paul Packer, September 11, 1940, Hancher Faculty Vertical File folder 1.
12. Untitled news clipping, *Cedar Rapids Gazette*, September 5, 1940, Hancher Faculty Vertical File folder 2.
13. Bob Estabrook, "Personal Opinion," *Cedar Rapids Gazette*, March 15, 1942.
14. Persons, *The University of Iowa in the Twentieth Century*.
15. Pete Hoyt, "Would Rescind Hancher Election," *Cedar Rapids Gazette*, October 21, 1940.
16. Pope Ballard & Loos to Dr. Sumner Chase, October 26, 1940, Hancher Faculty Vertical File folder 1.
17. Ibid.
18. Thomas Tighe v. Victory Corporation, et al., 39S-11561 (Chancery Files of The Superior Court of Cook County, Illinois).
19. Pete Hoyt, "Would Rescind Hancher Election," *Cedar Rapids Gazette*, October 21, 1940.
20. Associated Press, "State Board Members Stand By President-Elect of S.U.I.," *Daily Iowan* (State University of Iowa, Iowa City), October 22, 1940.
21. Paul De Camp, "Virgil M. Hancher Goes Into 10th Year as Head of S.U.I.," *Iowa City Press-Citizen*, November 1, 1949.
22. "Iowa Stadium Out of Financial Rough," *Ames Tribune*, December 4, 1940.
23. "The President and the University: 1940-60," *Iowa Alumni Review*, June 1960, 4.
24. Virgil M. Hancher to Members of the State Board of Regents and Finance Committee, November 5, 1963, box 536 folder 6, Virgil M. Hancher Papers, The University of Iowa Libraries, Iowa City, Iowa.
25. Janet Haven, "Introduction," *Going Back to Iowa: The World of Grant Wood*, http://xroads.virginia.edu/~MA98/haven/wood/intro.html
26. Persons, *The University of Iowa in the Twentieth Century*.

27. John C. Gerber, *A Pictorial History of the University of Iowa* (Iowa City: University of Iowa Press, 1988).
28. N.G. Alcock, "Medic Plan Creates Rift," *Daily Iowan*, August 15, 1947.
29. E. Bruce Hughes, "Hancher Says Plan is Not Socialistic," *Daily Iowan*, August 15, 1947.
30. Iid.
31. Virgil M. Hancher to Members of the State Board of Regents and Finance Committee, November 5, 1963, box 536 folder 6, Virgil M. Hancher Papers, The University of Iowa Libraries, Iowa City, Iowa.
32. Dr. Fred Stamler, "Department of Pathology: Departmental History," University of Iowa Carver College of Medicine, http://www.medicine.uiowa.edu/pathology/aboutus/history/
33. "Open Handicapped Children's Hospital School," *Mason City Globe-Gazette*, October 11, 1948.
34. "Nurse School Now Ranks as a 'U' College," *Kossuth County Advance*, December 6, 1949.
35. "University of Iowa Enters 100th Year, Future is Bright," *University of Iowa News Bulletin*, March 1946.
36. Persons, *The University of Iowa in the Twentieth Century*.
37. "The President and the University: 1940-60," *Iowa Alumni Review*, June 1960, 4.
38. G.E. Whitehead, "Legislative News: From the Senate," *The Bayard News*, March 31, 1949.
39. United Press International, "Governor Cuts Asking of Board of Education," *Daily Iowan*, January 25, 1949.
40. Dwight G. Rider, "The President: Administrator," Iowa *Alumni Review*, June 1960, 12.
41. State University of Iowa, "Reconciliation of State Auditor's Report as of February 28, 1949 and the University Estimate Made in September 1948," April 11, 1949, Hancher papers box 221, folder 85.
42. S.U.I. Balance of 2 Millions (reprint from April 9, 1949 *Des Moines Register*), Hancher papers box 221, folder 85.
43. "Order Investigation At Iowa U: Attack Made On University In Iowa House," *Mount Pleasant News*, April 13, 1949.
44. "Iowa House Drops Move For Investigation Of SUI," *Daily Iowan*, April 14, 1949.
45. "The Blind Attack on our University," *Des Moines Register*, April 16, 1949.
46. "Senate Passes School Budget," *Council Bluffs Nonpareil*, April 13, 1949.

47. Kingsley M. Clarke to Virgil M. Hancher, April 19, 1949 (as reprinted in April 23 State University of Iowa Information Service press release), Hancher papers box 221, folder 85.

48. George Mills, "Probe of S.U.I. is Voted Down," c. April 1949, Hancher papers box 221, folder 85.

49. Dwight G. Rider, "The President: Administrator," *Iowa Alumni Review*, June 1960, 12.

50. "Board of Education Appropriation Measure Goes on Senate Calendar," *Carroll Daily Times Herald*, April 12, 1946.

51. "Iowa Once Had Governors Who Believed in Education," *Mason City Globe-Gazette*, March 29, 1949 (reprinted on State University of Iowa School of Journalism letterhead), Hancher papers box 221, folder 85.

52. Dwight G. Rider, "The President: Administrator," *Iowa Alumni Review*, June 1960, 12.

53. Virgil M. Hancher to J. Kendall Lynes, April 4, 1950, Hancher Faculty Vertical File folder 1.

54. Mary Jane McLaughlin to Dean A.H. Scaff, February 28, 1972, Association of American Universities [RG01.15.04], Organizations and Clubs Vertical Files, The University of Iowa Libraries, Iowa City, Iowa.

55. Henry M. Wriston to Virgil M. Hancher, July 31, 1950, box 1.15 folder "Hancher: [committees] Membership 1949-51," Association of American Universities Records Ms. 197, Special Collections, Milton S. Eisenhower Library, The Johns Hopkins University.

56. Virgil M. Hancher to Henry M. Wriston, August 11, 1950, Association of American Universities Records box 1.15, "Hancher: [committees] Membership 1949-51" folder.

57. Reuben G. Gustavson to Virgil M. Hancher, July 3, 1950, Association of American Universities Records box 1.15, "Hancher: [committees] Membership 1949-51" folder.

58. Virgil M. Hancher to Henry M. Wriston, August 11, 1950, Association of American Universities Records box 1.15, "Hancher: [committees] Membership 1949-51" folder.

59. Virgil Hancher and Ralph Ellsworth, handwritten comments on invitation to University of Florida centennial, March 3, 1953, Hancher faculty vertical file folder 1.

60. Virgil M. Hancher to Frederick A. Middlebush, November 10, 1950, Association of American Universities Records box 1.15, "Hancher: [committees] Membership 1949-51" folder.

61. Persons, *The University of Iowa in the Twentieth Century*.

62. Virgil M. Hancher to Henry C. Shull (draft letter stamped "not sent"), October 22, 1948, Hancher papers box 221, folder 85.

CHAPTER 2

1. James G. Hilton, phone interview with the author, January 6, 2015.

2. James H. Hilton, "James. H. Hilton's Story from 1899-1965," box 1 folder 4, James H. Hilton Papers, RS 2/10, Special Collections Department, Iowa State University Library.

3. Ibid.

4. Raymond Lowery, "Tar Heel of the Week JAMES H. Hilton," ca. 1950, Hilton papers box 14, "HILTON, James H. #1" folder.

5. Hilton, "James. H. Hilton's Story from 1899-1965."

6. Ibid.

7. Ibid.

8. Ibid.

9. Ibid.

10. Phyllis Fleming, "Unique Loyalty at ISU: President Hilton Its Best Example," *Cedar Rapids Gazette*, October 7, 1962.

11. Hilton, "James. H. Hilton's Story from 1899-1965."

12. Ibid.

13. Lowery, "Tar Heel of the Week JAMES H. Hilton."

14. "The President and the University: 1940-60," *Iowa Alumni Review*, June 1960, 4.

15. Hilton, "James. H. Hilton's Story from 1899-1965."

16. Iowa State Board of Education, news release, November 6, 1952, Hilton papers box 14, "HILTON, James H. #1" folder.

17. Margaret Sloss, Transcript of farewell dinner for Dr. and Mrs. Hilton, March 22, 1965, Hilton papers box 1, folder 13.

18. Hilton, "James. H. Hilton's Story from 1899-1965."

19. Ibid.

20. Ibid.

21. "Hilton to Speak to State Alumni in Meeting Here," *The Robesonian* (Lumberton, NC), April 7, 1952.

22. Hilton, "James. H. Hilton's Story from 1899-1965."

23. "The President and the University: 1940-60," *Iowa Alumni Review*, June 1960, 4.

24. Hilton, "James. H. Hilton's Story from 1899-1965."

25. James H. Pou Bailey, "Raleigh Round-Up," *The Robesonian* (Lumberton, NC), November 22, 1950.

26. Hilton, "James. H. Hilton's Story from 1899-1965."

27. Iowa State Board of Education, news release, November 6, 1952, Hilton papers box 14, "HILTON, James H. #1" folder.

28. J.S. Russell, "They Hate to See Us Take Their 'Dr. Jimmie,'" *Iowa Farm and Home Register*, February 1, 1953.

29. Rex Conn, "Jim is Coming Back," *The Alumnus of Iowa State College*, January 1953.

CHAPTER 3

1. Stow Persons, *The University of Iowa in the Twentieth Century: An Institutional History* (Iowa City: University of Iowa Press, 1990).

2. Robert Underhill, *Alone Among Friends: A Biography of W. Robert Parks* (Ames: Iowa State University Press, 1999).

3. Ibid.

4. Gerald L. Peterson, "Brief History of UNI, 1876-1995," University of Northern Iowa Rod Library, last modified January 28, 2016, https://www.library.uni.edu/collections/special-collections/university-archives/brief-history-uni-1876-1995

5. Ibid.

6. Persons, *The University of Iowa in the Twentieth Century*.

7. Ibid.

8. "Hancher: SUI Needs About $2,500,000 Yearly More Than Legislators Considering," *Ames Tribune*, February 26, 1951.

9. "Iowa State: Report to Budget and Financial Control Committee," August 20, 1954, Hilton papers box 10, folder 29.

10. Dorothy Schweider, "Iowa State at Mid-Century: The Friley and Hilton Years," in *A Sesquicentennial History of Iowa State University: Tradition and Transformation*, ed. Schweider and Gretchen Van Houten (Ames: Iowa State University Press, 2007).

11. Rex Conn, "ISC Gets Quiet, Aggressive Leader: Method Is: Listen, See—Then Act," *Cedar Rapids Gazette*, July 12, 1953.

12. "James Hilton's Installation," Iowa State University Office of the President, http://www.president.iastate.edu/archives/12/install/hilton.php

13. "Athletics Will 'Improve' President Hilton Announces," *Iowa State Daily*, November 24, 1953.

14. James H. Hilton, "James. H. Hilton's Story from 1899-1965," Hilton Papers box 1, folder 4.

15. Ibid.

16. Raymond B. Allen to Virgil M. Hancher, July 4, 1951, Association of American Universities Records box 1.15, "Hancher: [committees] Membership 1949-51" folder.

17. "Humanologist," *Time*, July 7, 1952.

18. Jon Van, "Libraries Planned With People in Mind," *Des Moines Register*, November 12, 1972.

19. J.S. Russell, "They Hate to See Us Take Their 'Dr. Jimmie,'" *Iowa Farm and Home Register*, February 1, 1953.
20. Conn, "ISC Gets Quiet, Aggressive Leader."
21. Hilton, "James. H. Hilton's Story from 1899-1965."
22. Schweider, "Iowa State at Mid-Century: The Friley and Hilton Years."
23. State University of Iowa News and Information Service press release, February 8, 1964, Hilton papers box 13.
24. Dorothy Kehlenbeck, Interview with James H. and Lois Hilton, June 8, 1968, Hilton papers box 1, folder 13.
25. Hilton, "James. H. Hilton's Story from 1899-1965."

CHAPTER 4

1. James H. Hilton, "Staff Convocation," 1955, Hilton papers box 4, folder 55.
2. James H. Hilton, "James. H. Hilton's Story from 1899-1965," Hilton Papers box 1, folder 4.
3. "The Golf Lift Gab," *Daily Iowan*, February 14, 1956.
4. "Critics of Pressbox, Golf Lift, Criticized," *Daily Iowan*, November 28, 1957.
5. "University of Iowa President Stricken," *Logansport Pharos-Tribune* (Logansport, IN), November 21, 1956.
6. "Iowa U President Gets Too Excited," *Lincoln Star* (Lincoln, NE), November 18, 1956.
7. Paul De Camp, "Virgil M. Hancher Goes Into 10th Year as Head of S.U.I.," *Iowa City Press-Citizen*, November 1, 1949.
8. "Editorial of day: Welcome News: Hancher Back on Job," *Mason City Globe-Gazette*, February 25, 1957.
9. "University of Iowa President Stricken," *Logansport Pharos-Tribune* (Logansport, IN), November 21, 1956.
10. "Iowa Regents Relate Needs To Governor," *Carroll Daily Times Herald*, July 12, 1957.
11. James H. Hilton, "Staff Convocation," 1955, Hilton papers box 4, folder 55.
12. James H. Hilton, "Address to Staff Fall 1956," Hilton papers box 4, folder 55.
13. James H. Hilton, "Staff Convocation," 1957, Hilton papers box 4, folder 55.
14. "Pre-Audit Law Is Disregarded," *Council Bluffs Nonpareil*, February 19, 1955.
15. "Senate Votes to End Pre-Audit," *Iowa City Press-Citizen*, April 11, 1955.
16. "Political Ringside," *Carroll Daily Times Herald*, February 25, 1957.

17. James H. Jensen to Martin J. Nelson and Dr. Harvey Davis, November 19, 1956, Hilton papers box 4, folder 27.

18. Martin J. Nelson to Harvey Davis and James H. Jensen, April 27, 1956, Hilton papers box 4, folder 27.

19. Correspondence of Association of American Universities, Hancher papers box 385, folder 4D.

20. Virgil M. Hancher to James H. Hilton, January 9, 1958, box 5 folder 2, W. Robert Parks Papers, RS 2/11, Special Collections Department, Iowa State University Library.

21. James H. Hilton, "Closing Remarks: CENTENNIAL LUNCHEON: Great Hall, Memorial Union," March 22, 1958, Hilton papers box 10, folder 28.

22. Robert Underhill, *Alone Among Friends: A Biography of W. Robert Parks* (Ames: Iowa State University Press, 1999).

23. James H. Hilton, "Closing Remarks: CENTENNIAL LUNCHEON: Great Hall, Memorial Union," March 22, 1958, Hilton papers box 10, folder 28.

CHAPTER 5

1. Virgil M. Hancher to presidents and provosts, Memorandum re: "Suggestions on Future Directions for Development of Our Three Institutions," February 20, 1959, Hilton papers box 4, folder 21.

2. Ibid.

3. Virgil M. Hancher, "Observations on Problems of Growth in the Three State-Supported Institutions of Higher Education," March 5, 1959, Hancher Faculty Vertical File folder 1.

4. Hancher, "Suggestions on Future Directions for Development of Our Three Institutions."

5. Ibid.

6. Ibid.

7. James H. Hilton, "Some Reactions to President Hancher's Memorandum of March 5, 1959, Entitled 'Observations on Problems of Growth in the Three State-Supported Institutions of Higher Education,'" ca. April 1959, Hilton papers box 4, folder 21.

8. Ibid.

9. Ibid.

10. Ibid.

11. Stow Persons, *The University of Iowa in the Twentieth Century: An Institutional History* (Iowa City: University of Iowa Press, 1990).

12. "Review of Objectives of Iowa State College," Discussion at Meeting of Presidents and Provosts, Cedar Falls, September 30, 1958, Hilton papers box 4, folder 26.

13. Iowa State College, "ISC Presents Case for Name Change to ISU," draft news release, ca. 1959, Hilton papers box 2, folder 15.

14. David Hamilton, "Science with Humanity: The Parks Years," in *A Sesquicentennial History of Iowa State University: Tradition and Transformation*, ed. Dorothy Schweider and Gretchen Van Houten (Ames: Iowa State University Press, 2007).

15. Richard S. Bear to James H. Hilton, Memorandum re: "Revision of the Names of Iowa State College and of the Division of Science," ca. 1955, Hilton papers box 10, folder 25.

16. Iowa State College, "ISC Presents Case for Name Change to ISU."

17. "Reasons given by the Divisional faculties, students and alumni for changing the name of Iowa State College to Iowa STATE UNIVERSITY," ca. 1959, Hilton papers box 10, folder 25.

18. "Supplemental Information Concerning Change of Name of Iowa State," ca. 1959, Hilton papers box 10, folder 79.

19. James H. Hilton, handwritten note, ca. 1959, Hilton papers box 2, folder 15.

20. Iowa State College, "ISC Presents Case for Name Change to ISU."

21. "To Change the Name of the Institution," ca. 1959, Hilton papers box 10, folder 25.

22. James H. Hilton, handwritten note, ca. 1959, Hilton papers box 2, folder 15.

23. David McCartney, "What's in a name? For the University of Iowa, lots of history and a little confusion," Old Gold, *The Spectator*, December 2010, http://spectator.uiowa.edu/2010/december/oldgold.html

CHAPTER 6

1. Schweider, Underhill, and Hamilton.

2. James H. Hilton, "James. H. Hilton's Story from 1899-1965," Hilton Papers box 1, folder 4.

3. Virgil M. Hancher, draft document "If, by will or otherwise, I could leave one legacy…" ca. 1964, Hancher papers box 536, folder "No. 6A 1963-64."

4. Stow Persons, *The University of Iowa in the Twentieth Century: An Institutional History* (Iowa City: University of Iowa Press, 1990).

5. J. William Maucker to presidents and provosts (summary of March 14, 1959 presidents and provosts meeting, Fort Des Moines hotel), March 17, 1959, Hilton papers box 10, folder 25.

6. "ISC Renaming Decision Delayed," *Mason City Globe-Gazette*, March 13, 1959.

7. Maucker to presidents and provosts, March 17, 1959.

8. Paul Deaton, "50th anniversary of UI name change—or not," *Iowa City Press-Citizen*, October 21, 2014, http://www.press-citizen.com/story/news/education/university-of-iowa/2014/12/22/th-anniversary-ui-name-change/17702821
9. "Iowa State Wants a New Name," *Humboldt Republican*, March 18, 1959.
10. "Now We're Confused," *Humboldt Republican*, July 8, 1959.
11. "Iowa State Wants a New Name," *Humboldt Republican*, March 18, 1959.
12. "Should Iowa State be called a University," *Kossuth County Advance* (Algona), March 31, 1959.
13. "Iowa State Is a University," *Cedar Rapids Gazette*, February 25, 1959.
14. "Oppose ISC Name Change," *Ames Tribune*, April 11, 1959.
15. "Capitol News Letter," *Harlan Advertiser*, April 28, 1959.
16. Gene L. Hoffman to James H. Hilton, April 10, 1959, Hilton papers box 10, folder 79.
17. "Capitol Letter: Highlights and Sidelights Of Iowa State Legislature," *Sioux Center News*, May 7, 1959.
18. "ISC Name Change is Approved," *Ames Tribune*, May 5, 1959.
19. "Name Change Bill Signed; It's Iowa State University," *Iowa State Daily*, May 13, 1959.
20. Hilton, "James. H. Hilton's Story from 1899-1965."
21. "Name Change Bill Signed," *Iowa State Daily* , May 13, 1959.
22. "'College' Is Everywhere: Prepare for Name Change," *Ames Tribune*, June 27, 1959.
23. Ronald Rosmann to "the Dean of the University," February 16, 1964, Hilton papers box 8, folder 11.
24. Arthur W. Walsh to Ronald Rosmann, February 27, 1964, Hilton papers box 8, folder 11.
25. Mildred Beem to James H. Hilton, October 15, 1962, Hilton papers box 3, folder 24.
26. Bill Sherman, "SUI-ISU Mixup Proves Perplexing Postal Problem," *Daily Iowan*, October 12, 1962.
27. "Two Great Universities," *Mason City Globe-Gazette*, May 2, 1959.
28. "Capitol Letter," *Sioux Center News*, May 7, 1959.
29. "More and Moore… Timely Topics," *Winterset Madisonian*, August 5, 1959.

CHAPTER 7

1. "State Board Approves New Class At Teachers College," *College Eye* (Iowa State Teachers College, Cedar Falls), May 13, 1955.

NOTES TO PAGES 102-108

2. Helen R. LeBaron to Harold V. Gaskill, June 1, 1953, Hilton papers box 10, folder 46.
3. Iowa State College, "Report to Budget and Financial Control Committee," August 20, 1954, Hilton papers box 10, folder 29.
4. Interinstitutional Committee on Educational Coordination to Iowa State Board of Education, Memorandum re: "Vocational Home Economics," ca. 1954, Hilton papers box 10, folder 46.
5. J. William Maucker to Iowa State Board of Education, Memorandum re: "Comments on Report of Interinstitutional Committee Regarding Preparation of High School Teachers of Vocational Home Economics," ca. 1955, Hilton papers box 10, folder 46.
6. M.J. Nelson to Harold V. Gaskill and Harvey Davis, April 22, 1954, Hilton papers box 10, folder 46.
7. Interinstitutional Committee to State Board of Education, re: "Vocational Home Economics."
8. Maucker to State Board of Education, re: "Comments on... Preparation of High School Teachers of Vocational Home Economics."
9. James H. Hilton, "James. H. Hilton's Story from 1899-1965," Hilton Papers box 1, folder 4.
10. James H. Hilton, "Staff Convocation," September 8, 1964, Hilton papers box 14, folder 55.
11. Todd Stevens, *Cyclones Handbook: Stories, Stats and Stuff About Iowa State™ Football & Basketball* (Wichita, KS: The Wichita Eagle and Beacon Publishing Co., 1996).
12. James H. Hilton, "Address to the Staff: Great Hall Memorial Union," July 3, 1953, Hilton papers box 14, folder 55.
13. Iowa State College Department of English and Speech, "Problems Of Hiring Arising From the Fact that we Have no Major in English and Speech and no Graduate Program," ca. 1959, Hilton papers box 10, folder 25.
14. "English and Speech," analysis of Iowa State College curricula, ca. 1959, Hilton papers box 4, folder 26.
15. J. William Maucker to presidents and provosts (summary of March 14, 1959 presidents and provosts meeting, Fort Des Moines hotel) March 17, 1959, Hilton papers box 10, folder 25.
16. "Reasons for Iowa State's Offering Programs in the Social Sciences and Humanities," April 1959, Hilton papers box 12, folder 5.
17. "Review of Objectives of Iowa State College," Discussion at Meeting of Presidents and Provosts, Cedar Falls, September 30, 1958, Hilton papers box 4, folder 26.
18. James H. Hilton to Iowa Board of Regents, "LETTER," ca. 1960, Hilton papers box 10, folder 25.
19. Maucker to presidents and provosts, March 17, 1959.

NOTES TO PAGES 108-125

20. "Clash Over ISU, ISTC Expansion," *Ames Tribune*, April 14, 1960.
21. Virgil M. Hancher, "Some Problems of Higher Education," speech to School of Banking, Madison WI, August 22, 1960, Hancher papers, speeches box 14.
22. Ibid.
23. Harvey Davis, "Items of Contemplated Expansion at the State University of Iowa," October 19, 1959, Hilton papers box 14, folder 3.
24. Maucker to presidents and provosts, March 17, 1959.
25. Davis, "Items of Contemplated Expansion."
26. Ibid.
27. "SUI's Request for Vocational Home Economics," etc., ca. 1959, Hilton papers box 14, folder 3.
28. Ibid.
29. "Clash Over ISU, ISTC Expansion," *Ames Tribune*, April 14, 1960.
30. "ISU-SUI Alums Urge Hancher to Drop Opposition to English Majors Here," *Ames Tribune*, April 25, 1960.
31. "Iowa State request clarified by Hilton," *Mason City Globe-Gazette*, April 27, 1960.
32. Dorothy Schweider, "Iowa State at Mid-Century: The Friley and Hilton Years," in *A Sesquicentennial History of Iowa State University: Tradition and Transformation*, ed. Schweider and Gretchen Van Houten (Ames: Iowa State University Press, 2007).
33. James H. Hilton to W.C. Stuart, April 25, 1960, Hilton papers box 12, folder 6.
34. James H. Hilton to Irving Long, April 21, 1960, Hilton papers box 12, folder 6.
35. James H. Hilton to Robert Rigler, April 21, 1960, Hilton papers box 12, folder 6.
36. James H. Hilton, "Address to Staff," September 16, 1953, Hilton papers box 14, folder 55.
37. Hancher, "Some Problems of Higher Education."
38. Ibid.

CHAPTER 8

1. James H. Hilton, "Staff Convocation," 1955, Hilton papers box 14, folder 55.
2. James H. Hilton, "Staff Convocation," September 8, 1964, Hilton papers box 14, folder 55.
3. "The President and the University: 1940-60," *Iowa Alumni Review*, June 1960, 4.
4. J. William Maucker to presidents and provosts (summary of March 14, 1959 presidents and provosts meeting, Fort Des Moines hotel) March 17, 1959, Hilton papers box 10, folder 25.

5. Stow Persons, *The University of Iowa in the Twentieth Century: An Institutional History* (Iowa City: University of Iowa Press, 1990).

6. Mike Pauly, "Iowa Legislators Threaten to Slice Funds to Schools," *Daily Iowan*, January 28, 1961.

7. Robert Underhill, *Alone Among Friends: A Biography of W. Robert Parks* (Ames: Iowa State University Press, 1999).

8. David D. Dewey, "A Tribute by David D. Dewey," (pamphlet reprinting from Summer 1964 *Iowa Law Review*), Hancher Faculty Vertical File folder 2.

9. R.A. Morton, "Tribute to James H. Hilton," May 22, 1982, Hilton papers box 1, folder 9.

10. Iowa State Board of Education, news release, November 6, 1952, Hilton papers box 14, "HILTON, James H. #1" folder.

11. James G. Hilton, phone interview with the author, January 6, 2015.

12. C.A. Iverson, "Personal Visits with Legislators," 1961, Hilton papers box 5, folder 46.

13. James Beilman, "Oral History Interview with Susan Hancher," July 23, 1976, Special Collections Archives, The University of Iowa Libraries, Iowa City, Iowa.

14. Virgil Hancher, "The State University and American Dream," Remarks to National Association of State Universities Annual Meeting, Salt Lake City, May 3-4, 1954, Hancher Faculty Vertical File folder 2.

15. Persons, *The University of Iowa in the Twentieth Century*.

16. "The President and the University," *Iowa Alumni Review*.

17. Virgil Hancher to Earl J. McGrath, December 18, 1945, Hancher Faculty Vertical File folder 1.

18. "Humanologist," *Time*, July 7, 1952.

19. James H. Hilton, "Some Reactions to President Hancher's Memorandum of March 5, 1959, Entitled 'Observations on Problems of Growth in the Three State-Supported Institutions of Higher Education,'" ca. April 1959, Hilton papers box 4, folder 21.

20. Virgil M. Hancher, "Some Problems of Higher Education," speech to School of Banking, Madison WI, August 22, 1960, Hancher papers, speeches box 14.

CHAPTER 9

1. "Educators Tell Construction Needs—Schools Had 25 Lean Years, Barracks Wearing Out," *Carroll Daily Times Herald*, September 16, 1958.

2. Dennis Binning, "University Budget Askings Explained," *Daily Iowan* (State University of Iowa, Iowa City), February 26, 1963.

3. Virgil Hancher, "The State University and American Dream," Remarks to National Association of State Universities Annual Meeting, Salt Lake City, May 3-4, 1954, Hancher Faculty Vertical File folder 2.

4. Ned Disque to James Jordan (letter and attached radio script), June 16, 1958, Hilton papers box 10, folder 88.

5. Binning, "University Budget Askings Explained."

6. Richard "Dutch" Elder, et al., Q&A [early 1963], Hilton papers box 12, folder 41.

7. Virgil Hancher to James H. Hilton, et al., February 15, 1960, Hilton papers box 12, folder 10.

8. Ed Heins, "Problems Facing State's Colleges Told to Regents," *Ames Tribune*, January 1, 1960.

9. James G. Hilton, phone interview with the author, January 6, 2015.

10. James H. Hilton, "James. H. Hilton's Story from 1899-1965," Hilton Papers box 1, folder 4.

11. "Detailed Comments, With Supporting Evidence on Statements Made in 'The Educational Load Factor at the State University of Iowa,'" July 1962, Hilton papers box 10, folder 22.

12. Ibid.

13. Heins, "Problems Facing State's Colleges Told to Regents."

14. "State University of Iowa: Basic Assumptions," January 29, 1960, Hilton papers box 19, folder 42.

15. Carl Gernetzky, Minutes of Legislative Planning Committee Meeting, January 29, 1960, Hilton papers box 19, folder 42.

16. "SUI budget should be greater than Iowa State—Hancher," *Mason City Globe-Gazette*, April 19, 1960.

17. Virgil M. Hancher, "The Components of General Education," *The Journal of General Education*, October 1, 1946.

18. "Hilton in Capital: New role required of colleges," *Ames Tribune*, Oct. 19, 1961.

19. "SUI budget should be greater than Iowa State—Hancher," *Mason City Globe-Gazette*, April 19, 1960.

20. Ibid.

21. "Summary of President Hancher's Statements Made at the June Board Meeting," June 22, 1960, Hilton papers box 12, folder 10.

22. "SUI budget should be greater than Iowa State—Hancher," *Mason City Globe-Gazette*, April 19, 1960.

23. "Summary of President Hancher's Statements Made at the June Board Meeting," June 22, 1960, Hilton papers box 12, folder 10.

24. Roberta Fritchman, "Analysis of S.U.I. Cost Data and Ratios of Cost," July 1, 1960, Hilton papers box 10, folder 31.

25. Ibid.

26. "Comparison of State Appropriations 1959-61: SUI, ISU and ISTC," April 25, 1960, Hilton papers box 12, folder 10.

27. "Operating Budgets of the Three State Supported Institutions of Higher Learning," ca. 1960, Hilton papers box 12, folder 10.

CHAPTER 10

1. Virgil M. Hancher to Iowa Board of Regents, Memorandum re: "SUI Educational Load Factor and Board Decision of July 15, 1960," September 7, 1960, Hilton papers box 19, folder 43.

2. Ibid.

3. Ibid.

4. Virgil M. Hancher to Members of the Board of Regents and Finance Committee, March 15, 1960, Hilton papers box 19, folder 42.

5. James H. Hilton, "Analysis of the Paper Entitled 'Observations on Problems of Growth in the Three State Supported Institutions of Higher Learning,'" March 7, 1961, Hilton papers box 10, folder 25.

6. "Points of Tension: Alumni-Legislator Contact Program," November 1960, Hilton papers box 5, folder 46.

7. "Hancher Tells Needs of SUI in Union Trial," *Daily Iowan*, January 21, 1961.

8. "S.U.I. Leads Efforts Against Bias—Hancher," *Iowa City Press-Citizen*, May 8, 1962.

9. Mike Pauly, "Iowa Legislators Threaten to Slice Funds to Schools," *Daily Iowan*, January 28, 1961.

10. James H. Hilton, "The Appropriations Request," ca. 1960, Hilton papers box 2, folder 1.

11. "1961-63 Hearings Before Governor Erbe," Dec. 16, 1960, Hilton papers box 2, folder 1.

12. Mandy Easter, Iowa Law Library, e-mail message to author, October 12, 2015.

13. Todd Stevens, *Cyclones Handbook: Stories, Stats and Stuff About Iowa State™ Football & Basketball* (Wichita KS: The Wichita Eagle and Beacon Publishing Co., 1996).

14. Donald K. Smith, "Unless Present Athletic Situation Improves Iowa State Could Be Forced Out of Big Eight," *Ames Tribune*, September 2, 1959.

15. "ISU denies filing tv protest this season," *Ames Tribune*, October 4, 1961.

16. Ibid.

17. Ibid.
18. "Cyclones Stand Pat on Theater TV Plan," *Carroll Daily Times Herald*, October 4, 1961.
19. "Hilton says NCAA, not ISU decides telecast ban," *Ames Tribune*, October 6, 1961.
20. "Hilton Declines to Withdraw Objection," *Carroll Daily Times Herald*, October 9, 1961.
21. "Hilton says NCAA, not ISU decides telecast ban," *Ames Tribune*, October 6, 1961.
22. "Hilton Declines to Withdraw Objection," *Carroll Daily Times Herald*, October 9, 1961.
23. "Hilton's Stamp on Commencement," *Ames Tribune*, May 22, 1965.
24. James H. Hilton, "Appropriations Committee: 1961," Hilton papers box 12, folder 23.
25. James H. Hilton, "Faculty Convocation," September 5, 1961, Hilton papers box 14, folder 55.
26. James H. Hilton, "James. H. Hilton's Story from 1899-1965," Hilton Papers box 1, folder 4.
27. "Hancher Cites Iowa's Needs," *Daily Iowan*, January 27, 1961.

CHAPTER 11

1. James G. Hilton, phone interview with the author, January 6, 2015.
2. James H. Hilton, "James. H. Hilton's Story from 1899-1965," Hilton Papers box 1, folder 4.
3. [Roberta Fritchman?], "An Analysis of the SUI Educational Load Factor Study," January 28, 1961, Hilton papers box 19, folder 43.
4. Wayne R. Moore to James H. Hilton and B.H. Platt, Memorandum re: "Meeting of the Committee of Nine, March 2, 1961, Des Moines," March 3, 1961, Hilton papers box 19, folder 43.
5. Ibid.
6. "Minutes of Toledo Society Meeting," April 27, 1962, Hilton papers box 14, folder 31.
7. "Minutes of Toledo Society Meeting," May 29, 1962, Hilton papers box 14, folder 31.
8. James H. Hilton to Iowa Board of Regents, June 25, 1962, Hilton papers box 10, folder 23.
9. James Jordan to Virgil Hancher, June 25, 1962, Hancher papers box 536, "cost studies #1" folder.
10. Ibid.

11. "S.U.I.'s Position Regarding the 1960-61 Cost Study and Its Uses," ca. 1962, Hancher papers box 536, "COST STUDY" binder.

12. Jordan to Hancher, June 25, 1962.

13. "The State University of Iowa's Request for Operating Funds in Proportion to its Educational Load Factor," July 1960, Hancher papers box 536, "COST STUDY" binder.

14. "S.U.I.'s Position Regarding the 1960-61 Cost Study and Its Uses."

15. J. William Maucker to Iowa Board of Regents, "Comments on SUI Memo on Cost Study, June, 1962," July 5, 1962, Hancher papers box 536, "COST STUDY" binder.

16. James H. Hilton to Iowa Board of Regents, July 3, 1962, Hilton papers box 10, folder 22.

17. Harrison Weber, "Educational Load Factor is big issue for Iowa Regents," *Mason City Globe-Gazette*, July 18, 1962.

18. Harrison Weber, "ISU and SUI Battle Over State Fund," *Carroll Daily Times Herald*, July 19, 1962.

19. Harrison Weber, "SCI Says 'Load Factor' Defined by SUI to Apply to University Alone," *Carroll Daily Times Herald*, July 25, 1962.

20. "Impact of Unrecognized Load Factor: SUI PROGRAM DILUTION," ca. 1962, Hancher papers box 536, "COST STUDY" binder.

21. "Regents," *The Guthrian*, July 24, 1962.

22. James H. Hilton to Iowa Board of Regents, June 25, 1962, Hilton papers box 10, folder 23.

23. Wayne R. Moore to James H. Hilton, "University Cost Study Progress Report," October 11, 1961, Hilton papers box 19, folder 43.

24. Hilton, "James. H. Hilton's Story from 1899-1965."

25. Wayne R. Moore to James H. Hilton, "Progress Report on 1960-61 Cost Analysis" August 2, 1961, Hilton papers box 19, folder 43.

26. Wayne R. Moore to James H. Hilton, et al., October 26, 1962, Hilton papers box 14, folder 31.

27. Phyllis Fleming, "Unique Loyalty at ISU: President Hilton Its Best Example," *Cedar Rapids Gazette*, October 7, 1962.

28. Virgil Hancher to James H. Hilton and J. William Maucker, October 19, 1962, Hilton papers box 14, folder 31.

CHAPTER 12

1. Harrison Weber, "Overcrowding of Other Schools Cited—Legislative Unit to Study Feasibility of 4-Year State College in Western Iowa," *Carroll Daily Times Herald*, January 1, 1963.
2. Virgil Hancher to James H. Hilton and J. William Maucker, April 26, 1963, Hancher papers box 537, folder 6B.
3. Virgil Hancher to Iowa Board of Regents and Finance Committee, July 2, 1963, Hancher papers box 537, folder 6B.
4. Harold Hughes to Alfred W. Noehren, January 13, 1964, Hancher papers box 536, folder 6.
5. United Press International, untitled wire story, January 29, 1964, Hilton papers box 13, folder 71.
6. "Challenge to SUI," *Ames Tribune*, December 22, 1961.
7. "An extension budget for SUI," *Jefferson Herald*, January 18, 1962.
8. "Report of the Special Committee on the Extension Division," March 1960, Extension and Continuing Education Programs Records [RG 20/01], The University of Iowa Libraries, Iowa City, Iowa.
9. State University of Iowa analysis of extension services for Iowa Board of Regents, March 8, 1962, Extension and Continuing Education Programs Records.
10. "Hancher Looks at Future of University of Iowa," *Cedar Rapids Gazette*, February 2, 1964.
11. Ibid.
12. James H. Hilton, "I am sorry to have to disagree with President Hancher," January 29, 1964, Hilton papers box 13, folder 71.
13. Ibid.
14. Ibid.
15. Peter Van Zante to John T. Caldwell, January 31, 1964, Hilton papers box 13, folder 71.
16. John T. Caldwell to Peter Van Zante, February 5, 1964, Hilton papers box 13, folder 71.
17. Virgil M. Hancher, "Reminiscences," *Iowa Alumni Review*, June 1964, 5.
18. "Governor Hughes's press conference on 1/30/64," January 30, 1964, Hilton papers box 13, folder 17.
19. Ibid.
20. "Senate Heeds Suggestion; Strikes Center Fee Clause," *Iowa State Daily*, December 6, 1962.

21. Richard "Dutch" Elder, et al., Q&A [early 1963], Hilton papers box 12, folder 41.
22. State University of Iowa News and Information Service press release, February 8, 1964, Hilton papers box 13.
23. Iowa State University Information Service, "ISU Proposes Student Fee Increase," news release, February 13, 1964, Hilton papers box 5, folder 20.
24. Paul Smith, "Unfortunate temper display in regent-university row," *Kossuth County Advance*, March 5, 1964.
25. "Hancher protests delay in tuition ruling," *Mason City Globe-Gazette*, February 15, 1964.
26. Virgil Hancher and Ralph Ellsworth, handwritten comments on invitation to University of Florida centennial, March 3, 1953, Hancher faculty vertical file folder 1.
27. "Regents to Seek Added $38 Million," *Carroll Daily Times Herald*, June 20, 1964.
28. "Education costs are higher at Iowa State," *Mason City Globe-Gazette*, April 11, 1964.
29. Ibid.
30. Virgil Hancher to James H. Hilton and J. William Maucker, March 1, 1964, Hancher papers box 20, folder 48.
31. Jack Magarrell, "Regents Ask Budget Rise of One-Third," *Des Moines Register*, August 8, 1964.

CHAPTER 13

1. "The President and the University: 1940-60," *Iowa Alumni Review*, June 1960, 4.
2. "Regents Name Hancher SUI President Emeritus," *Daily Iowan*, August 8, 1964.
3. The University of Iowa Alumni Association, "Virgil M. Hancher, 18BA, 24JD, 64LLD," Distinguished Alumni Awards, http://www.iowalum.com/daa/search/profile.cfm?ID=344
4. James H. Hilton, "Staff Convocation," September 8, 1964, Hilton papers box 14, folder 55.
5. Jack Magarrell, "Regents Ask Budget Rise of One-Third," *Des Moines Register*, August 8, 1964.
6. Paul Deaton, "50th anniversary of UI name change—or not," *Iowa City Press-Citizen*, October 21, 2014, http://www.press-citizen.com/story/news/education/university-of-iowa/2014/12/22/th-anniversary-ui-name-change/17702821
7. "Two Great Universities," *Mason City Globe-Gazette*, May 2, 1959.
8. Deaton, "50th anniversary of UI name change—or not."
9. "Regents Act to Change Name at SUI," *The Guthrian*, November 2, 1964.

10. "Rules Regents Lacked Power to Change Name," *Carroll Daily Times Herald*, December 16, 1964.

11. "Nobody's Going to Sue," *Muscatine Journal*, December 21, 1964.

12. "SUI President, Wife Depart for Meeting in New Delhi, India," *Daily Iowan*, November 29, 1949.

13. W. Earl Hall, "Eulogy for a Friend," *Iowa Alumni Review*, April 1965.

14. "The President and the University," *Iowa Alumni Review*.

15. "Virgil Hancher Dies in India," *Des Moines Register*, January 31, 1965.

16. "'Special presentation' marks Veishea opening," *Ames Tribune*, May 6, 1965.

17. Robert Underhill, *Alone Among Friends: A Biography of W. Robert Parks* (Ames: Iowa State University Press, 1999).

18. David Hamilton, "Science with Humanity: The Parks Years," in *A Sesquicentennial History of Iowa State University: Tradition and Transformation*, ed. Dorothy Schweider and Gretchen Van Houten (Ames: Iowa State University Press, 2007).

19. Hilton, "Staff Convocation," September 8, 1964, Hilton papers box 14, folder 55.

20. "Dr. Hilton Resigns Post at I.S.U.," *Des Moines Register*, March 22, 1967.

21. James H. Hilton, "Address to the Staff," 1953, Hilton papers box 14, folder 55.

22. Iowa Public Television, "C.Y. Stephens Auditorium – 'Iowa Building of the Century,'" Iowa Pathways, http://www.iptv.org/IowaPathways/mypath.cfm?ounid=ob_000346

23. Underhill, *Alone Among Friends*.

24. Ibid.

25. Iowa State University Information Service, "Coliseum at Iowa State Center Named for James H. Hilton," news release, June 5, 1970, Hilton papers box 14, folder "HILTON, James #2."

26. James G. Hilton, phone interview with the author, January 6, 2015.

27. The University of Iowa News Services, "In 25 years Hancher has built an international reputation for innovation," news release, August 29, 2997, http://news-releases.uiowa.edu/1997/august/829hancher.html

28. B.A. Morelli, "Virgil Hancher," *Iowa City Press-Citizen*, March 11, 2010.

29. "Dr. Hilton Resigns Post at I.S.U.," *Des Moines Register*, March 22, 1967.

30. James G. Hilton, e-mail message to author, October 13, 2015.

CHAPTER 14

1. John "Buck" Turnbull, "No. 3 Tigers take on ISU, Hilton magic," *Des Moines Register*, February 14, 1989.

2. Kevin Trahan, "Iowa State proves Hilton Magic is real in breakthrough win over Kansas," *SB Nation*, January 18, 2015, http://www.sbnation.com/college-basketball/2015/1/18/7644845/iowa-state-kansas-big-12-hilton-gameday

3. Ned Disque to Stanley Yates, December 3, 1979, Hilton paper box 1, folder 2.

4. W. Robert Parks, "Portion of Remarks Made by W. Robert Parks at Hilton Banquet, March 22, 1965," Hilton papers box 14, folder "HILTON, James #2."

5. Stow Persons, *The University of Iowa in the Twentieth Century: An Institutional History* (Iowa City: University of Iowa Press, 1990).

6. James H. Hilton, "James. H. Hilton's Story from 1899-1965," Hilton Papers box 1, folder 4.

7. David Hamilton, e-mail message to author, January 15, 2015.

8. "The President and the University: 1940-60," *Iowa Alumni Review*, June 1960, 4.

9. Hilton, "James. H. Hilton's Story."

10. "Virgil Hancher Dies in India," *Des Moines Register*, January 31, 1965.

11. David Hamilton, "Science with Humanity: The Parks Years," in *A Sesquicentennial History of Iowa State University: Tradition and Transformation*, ed. Dorothy Schweider and Gretchen Van Houten (Ames: Iowa State University Press, 2007).

12. "Memorial Union addition is ready for occupancy," *Mason City Globe-Gazette*, July 3, 1965.

13. Hilton, "James. H. Hilton's Story."

14. Virgil M. Hancher, draft document "If, by will or otherwise, I could leave one legacy…" ca. 1964, Hancher papers box 536, folder "No. 6A 1963-64."

15. David Hamilton, e-mail message to author, January 15, 2015.

16. Persons, *The University of Iowa in the Twentieth Century*.

17. Massachusetts Institute of Technology, "Education," http://web.mit.edu/education/

18. Iowa Board of Regents, "Academic Policies and Procedures," chap. 6 in Iowa Board of Regents Policy Manual, http://www.regents.iowa.gov/Policies/Chapter 6/Chapter 6.pdf

19. Herman Quirmbach, e-mail message to author, October 27, 2015.

20. Hilton, "James. H. Hilton's Story."

INDEX

A

agriculture 2, 31, 38–39, 53, 55, 73, 75, 79, 81, 106, 119, 126, 148, 149, 189, 235
Agriculture Experiment Station 148–149
alumni 5, 17, 21, 27, 54, 78, 85, 89, 100, 115, 116, 155, 158, 164, 197, 210, 215
Ames, Iowa 4, 10, 11, 43, 53, 55, 63, 75, 83, 87, 93, 96, 100, 208, 209, 219
Ames Lab 32, 33–34, 75
appropriations 27–29, 32, 34, 64, 70, 78, 125, 129, 133, 135–138, 140–141, 143–146, 148, 152, 155–156, 157, 158, 163, 164, 169, 179, 181, 197, 203, 207, 225, 227, 235–236
Association of American Universities 30–34, 61, 73, 83, 99, 188, 211, 226
athletics 3, 7, 11–12, 22, 54, 59, 70, 71, 106, 159–162, 215, 221
audit of SUI. *See* free balance scandal

B

baby boom 129, 198
Beardsley, Gov. William 26, 27, 29, 49, 57, 70
Big Eight Conference 159, 161
Big Ten. *See* Western Conference
Bloody Thursday 29–30
Bowen, Howard 206, 207, 209, 211, 212
budgets 5, 26–27, 29, 34, 49, 54, 58, 63–64, 71, 102–103, 125, 135–141, 143–144, 145, 151, 152, 155–156, 157, 164, 172, 173–177, 179–181, 184, 197–204, 206, 227
Butler, Lamb, Foster and Pope. *See* Pope & Ballard

C

Caldwell, John 195
California and Western Conference study 145, 147–148, 149, 154
capital budgets 58, 70–71, 135–136, 217, 226
Cardinal Guild 73
cars, student-owned 68, 121–122
Cedar Rapids Gazette 19–20, 69, 94
Chicago 13, 16, 17, 18, 20, 25, 119
Clarke, Kingsley M. 27–28

Cold War 61, 71, 104–105
college rankings 62, 79, 180–181, 233
Committee of Nine 171, 182–183, 201
Constitution of Iowa 2, 86, 88, 93, 97–98, 209
cost studies 173–179, 181, 182, 183, 202. *See also* Committee of Nine
curriculum 61, 77, 79, 81, 83, 96, 100, 108–119, 129–131, 188, 213. *See also* English and speech degrees; *See also* nuclear engineering; *See also* vocational home economics
Cyclones 11, 59, 68, 106, 159–160, 216, 221

D

Davis, Harvey 112, 113, 114, 193
Deford, Frank 3–4, 8
Des Moines Register 69, 207, 212, 221
Dillon, Robert 160–161
Disque, N.E.D. 222
divisions vs. colleges 83–84, 92, 101
duplication 55–58, 65, 71, 73, 77, 78, 81, 82, 89, 101–103, 108, 113, 115, 117, 128–131, 133, 138, 156, 189, 191, 192, 196, 232, 234–235, 237

E

Educational Load Factor 139–142, 143–146, 147–150, 151–154, 155, 164, 169–171, 173–174, 175–181, 184, 188, 192, 196, 201–203, 206, 231
    Iowa State responses 139, 147–150, 153, 154, 169, 173, 174, 181
    media coverage 141, 179–180, 201
    State College of Iowa responses 174, 180–181, 184
engineering 55, 71, 78, 81, 83, 110, 131, 235. *See also* nuclear engineering
English and speech degrees 99, 107–109, 113, 115–118, 129, 156, 237
enrollments 5, 22, 26–27, 29, 54, 81, 117, 129, 135–136, 137, 141, 145, 148, 155, 164, 184, 187, 198, 213, 226, 233
extension services 2, 42, 45, 47, 79, 126, 156, 189–193, 195, 199, 228, 232
    controversies 2, 156, 189–197, 199, 228, 232

F

faculty salaries 24–25, 27–28, 58, 63, 79, 81–82, 136–139, 142, 148, 163, 224, 227
Farm Bureau 46
Farm Union 46
financial anemia 176, 180
football 54, 59–61, 70, 71, 106, 159–162
fraternities 13, 157
free balance scandal 27, 29
Friley, Charles 32–34, 51, 58
Fritchman, Roberta 147–149, 169
fundraising 64, 164, 197, 236
Future Directions memos 76–84, 103–104, 105, 131, 141, 147, 155, 188, 194

G

golf lift 69, 72
grants 85, 102, 103, 136, 219, 236
graphic design 7, 233
Grinnell College 206, 209

H

Hall, W. Earl 15–16, 17, 18, 21, 29, 212
Hamilton, David 6, 226, 227, 230
Hancher 1–2, 4–7, 8, 11, 13–35, 38, 45, 50, 57–58, 61, 64, 67–70, 72–74, 75–80, 81–82, 86, 88, 91–93, 94, 98, 99, 108–111, 115, 117–119, 121–125, 128–134, 135, 136, 139–148, 150, 151–154, 156–157, 164, 167, 172, 173–175, 177–179, 182, 184, 187–204, 205–207, 209, 210–213, 217–218, 222
 and legislators 6, 26–30, 31–32, 72, 78, 91, 125, 128–129, 133–134, 135–136, 143, 157, 164, 188–189, 211, 227, 236
 appointment to presidency 13, 17–20, 21, 30, 50
 as college student 14
 family 14, 17–19, 212
 heart attacks 6, 69–70, 72, 212
 history's verdict 6, 21, 25, 99, 125, 205, 212–213, 224, 235–237
 law career 13, 16–18, 20
 on liberal eduation 237
 on liberal education 61, 77, 108, 119, 131–132, 142, 145, 230
 personal qualities 8, 14–16, 21, 30, 33, 61, 80, 99, 111, 119, 121–125, 128, 132, 142, 146, 152, 157, 188, 199, 213, 224–230
 retirement 151, 184, 196, 205, 211
Hancher Auditorium 5, 64, 198, 217
Hancher, Dr. John W 14
Hancher - Hilton conflict 2–3, 6–7, 68, 74, 76–84, 86, 91, 92, 99, 107–111, 115, 118–119, 126–134, 139, 142–148, 150, 153–155, 158, 164, 167–169, 172–183, 184, 187–204, 206–207, 213, 217, 222–239
 comparison of participants 73, 80, 108, 111, 115, 123–129, 142, 146–147, 153, 164, 167–169, 196–199, 212–213, 222–232, 236–238
 personal dimension 6, 73, 78, 99, 167–169, 226–231
Hancher, Melvin Park 14
Hancher, Susan 17–19, 212
Hawkeyes 7, 11, 22, 70, 71, 159–161
Hilton Coliseum 5, 215, 221–222
Hilton, James G 37, 48, 126, 167–169, 216
Hilton, James H. 2, 5–7, 9, 37–53, 53, 57, 58–61, 62–65, 67–69, 71, 73, 75, 80–89, 91–93, 94–97, 100, 102, 104–109, 111–115, 115–118, 123, 125–127, 128, 129, 131, 132–133, 135–136, 138–144, 146–148, 149–150, 151, 153–156, 157–159, 161–163, 167–168, 171, 172, 177–179, 181–183, 184, 187–188, 190, 191, 193–204, 207, 210, 212–217, 221–223, 224–233, 235–237
 and legislators 48–49, 63, 71, 95, 116–117, 126–127, 129–130, 138, 157–159, 162–163, 178, 184, 223, 227, 236
 appointment to presidency 50, 58
 as college student 2, 37–38, 39, 42
 family 14, 38–43, 47, 50, 52, 126, 162, 168, 216, 219
 memoir 37, 51, 91, 182, 217, 227, 228, 237
 personal qualities 37, 40, 45, 46, 49, 62, 64, 67, 80, 82, 84, 106, 117, 123–126, 129, 142, 146, 158, 163–164, 167–169, 194, 222–226, 228, 236–237
 retirement 37, 182, 196, 198, 213–218, 236
Hilton, Lois Baker 46–47, 219
Hilton Magic 5, 221
his rival 223–238
hog barn 37–38, 42, 163
Homecoming protest, ISC 59
home economics 55, 78, 100–103, 106, 131, 149, 219, 232. *See also* vocational home economics
Hughes, Gov. Harold 189, 190, 193, 195–196
Hughes, Raymond 180
Hultman, Evan 210
humanities 80, 99, 107–108, 116, 232, 235. *See also* liberal education

I

India 211
influenza epidemic, 1918 42, 225
information technology 182, 231, 234
interinstitutional coordination 2, 73, 76, 79, 118, 172, 192
investigation of SUI 27–30
Iowa Board of Education 12, 13, 17, 19–20, 21, 29–30, 34, 50–52, 55–59, 83, 101, 103, 128, 130, 226, 234. *See also* Iowa Board of Regents

INDEX

Iowa Board of Regents 1, 12, 69, 71, 73, 76, 79, 89, 92–93, 96, 98, 106, 107, 111, 117–118, 130–131, 133, 135, 137–139, 140–141, 143–145, 150, 151–154, 156, 163, 164, 170–174, 179–182, 187, 188, 191–192, 193, 195–203, 205, 207, 210, 214, 225, 228, 235. *See also* Iowa Board of Education; *See also* Iowa Board of Education
   Hancher criticism 77, 130, 132, 192, 199, 229
Iowa City, Iowa 1, 4, 7, 10, 11, 14–15, 53, 55, 94, 156, 205, 209, 228
Iowa General Assembly. *See* Iowa legislature
Iowa legislature 6, 27–29, 32, 55, 56, 57, 70, 72, 78, 89, 93, 95–97, 116–117, 125, 126, 129, 133, 137, 138, 139, 145, 151, 152, 155–158, 162, 163, 171, 174, 177, 179, 184, 207, 210, 224, 227, 236
   funding for education. *See* appropriations
Iowa Stadium 22, 69
Iowa State Center 63–65, 67, 104, 164, 197–198, 213, 215–217, 219, 222–223. *See also* Hilton Coliseum; *See also* Stephens Auditorium
Iowa State College. *See* Iowa State University
Iowa State College Ten Years From Now 63–64, 222. *See also* Iowa State Center
Iowa State Teachers College 12, 54–55, 73, 76, 77, 78–79, 100–104, 107, 113, 114, 117, 143–146, 154, 156, 170, 190, 208, 233. *See also* State College of Iowa
   name change 12, 154, 208, 209. *See also* names and name changes
Iowa State University 1–8, 11, 28–29, 31–35, 43–45, 51–52, 53, 55, 57, 58–60, 62–64, 67–69, 72–73, 75–90, 91–100, 99–110, 111–118, 121, 127, 131, 138, 139, 143–146, 147–150, 155–156, 158–164, 168–173, 174, 176, 178–180, 182–184, 188–190, 192, 194, 197–198, 200–204, 206–208, 213–216, 221–222, 226–231, 232–234, 237
   athletics 59, 68, 159–160, 216. *See also* Cyclones
   name change 11, 68, 75, 83–90, 91–99, 99, 107, 116, 127, 160, 192, 210, 230. *See also* names and name changes
   origins 53, 55, 77
ISU Foundation 197

J

Jordan, James 173–176, 183

K

Kruschev, Nikita 6, 104–105

L

Ladd, Mason 88
land-grant system 1–2, 31, 33, 48, 51, 53, 62, 67, 80, 84, 87, 108, 118, 126, 145, 189, 194, 236
Lange, Rep. Elmer F. 210
LeBaron, Helen 100–102, 104, 219
legislators 63
liberal arts college 54, 78, 108, 116, 117, 144, 146, 156, 206, 232
liberal education 109–111, 119, 128, 131–132, 142, 230, 237
Loveless, Gov. Herschel 70, 71, 97

M

Massachussetts Institute of Technology (MIT) 79, 80, 235
Medical Service Plan 24–25, 224
mediocrity 82, 102, 108, 175, 233
Moore, Wayne 182
Morrill Act 53. *See also* land-grant system

N

names and name changes 4, 11–12, 55, 68, 75, 83–99, 107, 116, 127, 154, 160, 192, 208–211, 230
National Collegiate Athletics Association (NCAA) 160–161
newspaper coverage 19, 29, 58, 59, 69–70, 88, 93–95, 98, 115, 141, 169, 180, 195, 200–201, 205, 211–213
North Carolina 38, 41, 43, 48–49, 51, 63, 117, 193, 214, 219, 223. *See also* North Carolina State College
North Carolina State College 2, 37, 41–44, 48–49, 50–53, 62, 193, 195
Northwestern University 15, 17
nuclear engineering 112–113, 118, 133, 232
nursing 26, 62

O

O'Malley, Sen. George 69, 72, 95, 162
Oxford. *See* University of Oxford

P

Packer, Paul 19–20
panty raid 6, 68
Parks, Robert W. 84, 215, 223, 227–230
patriotism controversy 125, 157
Persons, Stow 92, 93, 125, 206, 224, 227, 230
Pope & Ballard 17, 20
pre-auditing 30, 58, 71–72, 128, 210
presidents & provosts meetings 92, 112, 123
Purdue University 31, 33, 47–48, 87, 145, 148, 174

Putney, Lawrence 28

R

Reynolds Foundation 214, 219
Rigler, Sen. Robert 117, 156
Rolfe, Iowa 10, 14, 15
Rose Bowl 71

S

salaries. *See* faculty salaries
Schweider, Dorothy 116
service courses 57, 78, 81, 85, 107, 163, 237
Spedding, Dr. Frank 32
Startown Farm Life School 39–41
State College of Iowa 12, 154, 174, 174–176, 178, 180, 182, 183, 189, 191, 201, 206, 208, 209, 229, 231. *See also* Iowa State Teachers College
State University of Iowa 2, 4, 5–8, 11, 14–15, 16–20, 22–29, 32, 34, 53–56, 58, 64, 67, 69, 71, 72, 73, 77–79, 88–89, 91, 93, 96, 98, 103, 111–113, 118, 132–133, 139–141, 143–146, 148–150, 151–152, 154–160, 164, 169–179, 180–185, 188–191, 193–198, 201, 202, 205–207, 208–210, 213, 214, 217, 225, 226–227, 228, 232–235, 237
    athletics 3, 7, 11, 22, 69, 159–161. *See also* Hawkeyes
    College of Medicine 24–25, 224
    College of Nursing 26, 62
    Memorial Union 15, 17, 156, 205, 228
    name change 4, 11, 88, 92, 98, 208–212. *See also* names and name changes
    university hospital 29, 149
Stephens Auditorium 215
strengthening programs budget 200, 203
Student Army Training Corps 42
student fees 197. *See also* tuition

T

televised football controversy 160–161, 190
temporary buildings 135, 164
Tighe, Thomas 21
Time magazine 24, 61, 130
Toledo formula 137–142, 144–145, 150, 152–153, 178, 181, 202
tuition 136, 142, 197–198, 235–236
Turnbull, John "Buck" 221

U

United Nations 156
University of Iowa. *See* State University of Iowa
University of Northern Iowa 4, 12. *See also* Iowa State Teachers College
University of Oxford 16, 46, 78, 110, 123, 126
University of Wisconsin 47, 118, 160

university system 1, 4, 52, 79, 189, 192, 193, 195, 209, 229, 234
Uthoff, John 183

V

VEISHEA 8
Victory Corporation 20–21
vocational home economics 101–104, 107, 112, 113, 117–118, 133, 232, 237

W

Western Conference 58, 145
western Iowa college proposal 187
Wood, Grant 6, 24
World War I 16, 41–42
World War II 22, 41, 49, 135
Wriston, Henry M. 30–33

About the Author

Matt Kuhns grew up in Anamosa, Iowa, and is an honors graduate of Iowa State University. He currently operates an independent design practice as Modern Alchemy LLC. As a writer, his previous work includes *Brilliant Deduction: The Story of Real-Life Great Detectives* and *Cotton's Library*. He lives in Lakewood, Ohio.

www.ingramcontent.com/pod-product-compliance
Lightning Source LLC
Chambersburg PA
CBHW031946080426
42735CB00007B/282